Candle Crafting
From an Art to a Science

Candle Crafting
From an Art to a Science

William Nussle

SOUTH BRUNSWICK AND NEW YORK: A. S. BARNES AND COMPANY
LONDON: THOMAS YOSELOFF LTD

© 1971 by A. S. Barnes and Co., Inc.
Library of Congress Catalogue Card Number: 70-146769

A. S. Barnes and Co., Inc.
Cranbury, New Jersey 08512

Thomas Yoseloff Ltd
108 New Bond Street
London W1Y OQX, England

First Printing, October, 1971
Second Printing, April, 1972

ISBN 0-498-07863-9
Printed in the United States of America

To the memory
of S. W. Ferris,
who first introduced me
to the science of petroleum wax technology

Contents

Preface

Candles are now made in many sizes, types, and shapes; some are colored and some are perfumed. Religious use of candles, inherited from the past, is practiced as much today (if not more) than ever before. Candles have also become a part of social grace. They are lighted to welcome visitors, and dining by candlelight is popular. Colored candles of almost any size or shape imaginable may be made for use as part of a period style decoration. Actually, candles are more popular today and are used for a greater variety of purposes than in the past.

Candle production methods have been improved and modified. While original methods for making candles are still used, new ways have been invented. In early days candles were produced by repetitive dipping and cooling, or by hand forming a plastic sheet of wax around a wick. Modern candle production methods include machine molding, compression molding, and extrusion.

One purpose of this book is to provide an insight into the many methods that may be employed to produce candles. Some are rather simple and easy, others are mechanically more complex.

Many candle businesses have started as a hobby in the home. With increasing demand for unique candles, the hobby developed into full-scale commercial production. Simple methods are described here for use by the home candle crafter. The more complex mechanical methods are described for commercial candle production.

Custom-made petroleum waxes have made a wide variety of candle types possible. Original candle fuels were restrictive for candle use. Specialized candle wicking has replaced original crude cotton wicking.

Waxes and wicks are described and defined, and sources of supply are given. Balance between wax, wick, and candle type is discussed, while technical details may be postponed until that stage of interest is reached.

Candles have had an interesting history, thus the background to the development of candles is presented. Candle production has expanded from a home craft as originally practiced to high production rate in large modern candle manufacturing plants. Modern scientific technology has made this expansion possible. Once again candle crafting has again returned to the home as a hobby or as a money making project for groups and organizations.

It is with home production of candles, as well as with the modern candle manufacturing plant in mind, that this book has been written. A comprehensive discussion of candle crafting is presented in simple terms for the hobbyist. The technical sections in each chapter are included for use, as the need develops, by the maturing candle maker and by the commercial candle manufacturer.

Whether you make plain or fancy candles, candle making is an enjoyable and profitable business.

The author gives credit to the many years of experience enjoyed as a wax technologist and service to the candle industry while employed by the Atlantic Richfield Company. Many thanks are given to fellow employees for advice and good counsel during the years this experience was gained.

Special thanks are given to Mr. W. R. Turner who made original sales service experience possible, to Mr. D. S. Brown for guidance and criticism when candle work was performed, and to Mr. Hugh McCaffery who did much of the investigative work. The suppliers of photographs used as illustrations in this book are gratefully acknowledged and credited.

Candle Crafting
From an Art to a Science

It is the simple things in life
that when put together
make life worthwhile.

1
Background to the Development of Candles

A candle may be defined as a wick surrounded by solidified fuel, which is burned to produce light.

Man from the beginning of time has consciously and subconsciously been attracted to light as a symbol and source of wisdom and knowledge. The sun and fire have had their place in religious worship, as have burnt offerings. As wisdom was gained through the ages, man was said to have seen the light and been enlightened —a very descriptive analogy.

Light has also had aesthetic significance, as well as benefits for illumination to displace darkness. The absence of light is darkness. Without control of light man lived in comparative ignorance and darkness. That period of time in man's development has appropriately been termed the Dark Ages. Light and knowledge went hand in hand. With gain in knowledge man became more and more able to control his environment. Control of fire and light were among his first accomplishments. Fire produced light, and with control of fire, light was provided for use where wanted and needed. In this way light grew into man's mental, spiritual, and physical being. The light of wisdom and the lamp of knowledge are recognized analogies.

The lamp and the candle were developed as an improvement upon the wood-knot previously used for illumination. Candles were at first given religious use, which has been retained to present day. It is thus not surprising that through religious application, along with aesthetic-utilitarian uses, the candle has retained favor.

Many religious faiths have the custom of using lighted candles for worship. In a Catholic Mass the lighted candle is a symbol of joy and a mark of reverence for the presence of Jesus Christ at the altar. In Leviticus, Chapter 6, Verse 12, appears the following command: "The fire is to be kept burning continuously on the altar, it must not go out." The votive light is used as a religious expression of prayer, adoration, veneration, thanksgiving, reparation, or petition, as intended by the one who lights the candle. It may also be used as a flaming tribute to God and the Saints. As such, custom requires the votive candle to burn seven days.

In the Jewish faith candles are burned in religious fashion on many occasions. Prior to the Sabbath, or on a holiday eve, two or more candles are lighted to symbolize the eve of a special day. These candles should burn until the evening meal is finished. Candles lighted on a Sabbath eve are to provide light through to the next day.

A tumbler candle is burned by the Jewish family on the anniversary of the death of a close member of the family. It may also be burned for special memorial services or on holidays such as Passover, Tabernacle Day, Pentecost or the Day of Atonement (Yom Kippur). These candles are to burn 24 hours.

It is Jewish custom that a family goes into mourning for seven days after the death of a member. During this period a Shiva candle is burned. This candle is made of pure white paraffin wax poured in a glass jar, and is similar to the Catholic seven day candle.

One of the more important candles in the Jewish religion is the Chanukah (Hanukkah) candle. It resembles a large birthday candle. It is burned to commemorate the anniversary of the Jewish rebellion against the Romans in Israel. Chanukah candles are burned in sequence; one on the first day, two on the second day, and so forth until eight candles are burned on the eighth day. The center candle is used to light the side candles.

At the end of a holiday, Jews ask for a blessing by prayer and light a Havdalah candle. This candle is unique in that it must have a multiple wick and is usually made by twisting two or more candles together.

Candles are burned in many Protestant churches to celebrate special occasions including Christmas, Easter, and weddings. Many religious candles are required to burn a specified length of time, and the science of candle making has made required burning time possible, as shown in following chapters.

Hanukka Candelabra (Courtesy George Arold, Hatfield, Pa.)

The candle may be traced back in time to the torch, which was a type of wick that self-contained the material used as fuel. However, precise dates in candle development are not known. Early candle forms were made by hand and included Links, Flambeaux, Rushlights, and Tapers. It is reasonably certain that some or all of these devices were used during the first century A.D. Sequence in development of the candle is vague. Obviously production of any one lighting device depended upon local availability of materials for wicking and fuel.

The Link was an improvement over the pine-knot torch. It was a rope of dried vegetable fibers saturated with fats, natural resins, tar, natural waxes, or mixtures thereof. The Flambeaux,

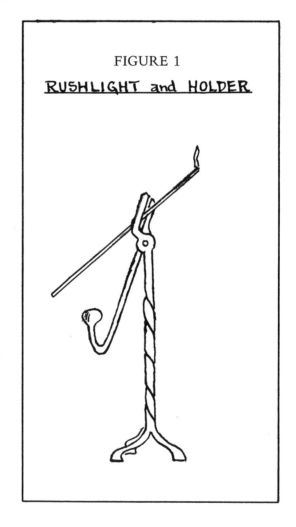

FIGURE 1

RUSHLIGHT and HOLDER

which may be considered an improvement on the Link, was a rough type of candle in which several fuel-saturated ropes, side by side, were sealed by heat, and over which more fuel was poured and then allowed to solidify.

Rushlights were candle-like devices in which the pith of rushes, reeds, and grasses were used as wicks. The rush stalk was prepared for use as a wick by removing all but one strip of the hard outer layer (cortex). This strip acted as a support for the soft inner pith. The prepared rush-wick was then soaked in melted fat or grease. If the fat was liquid at room temperature a rushlight was made. If the fat used was solid at room temperature, repeated dippings were made to prepare a rush candle of larger diameter. In burning a rushlight, it was held at an angle from the vertical, using a stand with a tongs or a pair of pliers to hold the light. As the rushlight burned it was moved up in the holder. Rush-candles—being larger in diameter and self-supporting—were burned in a vertical position. Since the pith was consumed in the flame there was no need for trimming the wick of the rushlight or rush candle. A typical rushlight is shown in Figure 1.

Candles were made to be an improvement over Rushlights and Flambeaux. Candles were originally made of a crudely twisted cotton wick, surrounded by a major portion of fuel, solid at room temperature. Greaseless stearine, bayberry wax, beeswax, and spermaceti were among the principal fuels used.

In comparison to the homemade rushlight, wax candles were a luxury; thus, during the Colonial period only the wealthy could afford them. It remained for the discovery of petroleum wax to make inexpensive candles readily available.

The Taper as a type of candle has had many forms. In some instances it was a large molded candle with either a tapered or a pyramid shape. A slender candle made in great lengths was also called a taper. This later type was made in a continuous process in which the candle was built up on the wick in layers. Starting with a long length of cotton wick, repeated passes were made through melted wax. After each pass, the wax solidified into an additional layer. In use, the slender taper was either formed into a coil, wrapped onto a spool, or cut into small lengths. In each form it was burned in a specially designed taper holder as shown in Figure 2.

In the early days of candle making many homemade candles performed poorly. The twisted cotton wick originally used had

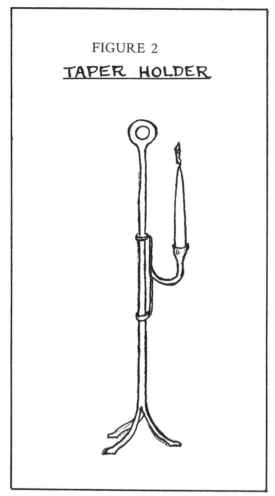

FIGURE 2

TAPER HOLDER

faults. It was non-uniform, it thickened with non-combustible residue from the candle fuel, and the tip of the wick was not consumed in the flame. The flame thus increased in size. Accumulation of a carbonaceous residue in the wick resulted in a smoky flame. If the non-combustible residue plugged the wick, the flame would be reduced to a feeble size. With either type of performance, the wick had to be shortened and trimmed frequently. It is of interest to note that the charred wick-end was termed snuff and the instrument used to remove the char, or to trim the wick, was referred to as a snuffer. It has been a common error to think of a candle snuffer as an extinguisher. Actually a snuffer was a scissor-like cutting instrument. It was not, however, uncommon to extinguish the flame when snuffing a burning candle and thus the confusion in terminology. In contrast to a candle snuffer, a candle extinguisher was a cone-shaped cap on the end of a rod. The cap would be placed over the flame to smother and thus extinguish it. A sketch of a candle snuffer and a candle extinguisher is shown in Figure 3.

Thanks to modern wicking and present day refined waxes, fault free candles may be made by proper wick and candle wax selection. Details on candle wicking are given in Chapter V. Wax and wick balance for a given type candle are discussed in several of the following chapters.

Development of present-day candle wax is of some interest. Lamps and candles appear to have had a common beginning: both are comprised of a suitable fuel and a wick. Original fuels included animal fats and oils, vegetable waxes, and insect waxes. Fuels that were liquid at ordinary use temperatures were contained in a holder to be burned as a lamp. Fuels that were solid at ordinary use temperatures were formed around a wick by one means or another and came to be known as candles. The term candle is derived from the latin word *candela,* which means glitter or flicker, and this is exactly how the original candles behaved.

Animal fats and oils that were used in lamps and candles included tallow, whale oil, lard oil, and spermaceti; vegetable waxes included bayberry wax and candelilla wax; and the principal insect wax has always been beeswax.

In about the middle of the 19th century, petroleum wax came

FIGURE 3

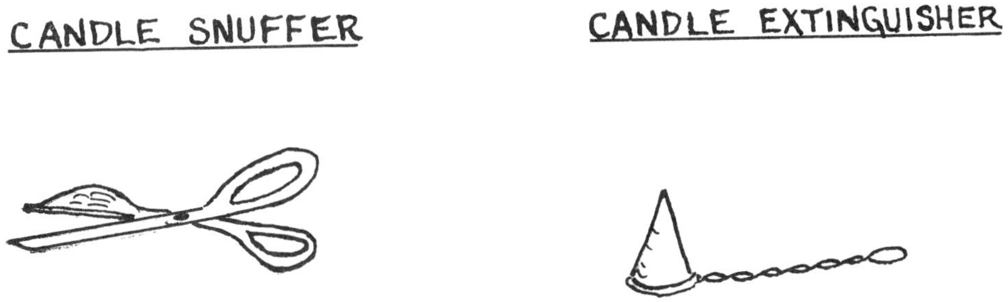

CANDLE SNUFFER   CANDLE EXTINGUISHER

into use for making candles. Because original petroleum wax was soft and plastic, stearic acid isolated from animal fat was developed for use as a hardening agent.

After the discovery of petroleum (rock oil), fractionation of the petroleum by distillation was learned. The kerosene fraction became a commercially important fuel for lamps, displacing the more expensive animal oils. By chilling and pressing the waxy distillate, wax was isolated and removed from it. Description of this operation and the modern improvements are discussed in detail in Chapter 4.

Petroleum wax refining is now a precise science. Oil-free white waxes having specified properties are conveniently made, and are now known as paraffin waxes. Petroleum refiners have rapidly increased their knowledge of paraffin wax, and with this knowledge they have improved facilities to meet the rapidly growing candle wax market. Thus, high quality paraffin waxes with specified properties have essentially displaced vegetable and insect waxes in candle use.

With precision control of properties, petroleum wax is now preferred for use in candle manufacture. Wax may be custom made for use in production of any specified type candle and required performance. Low cost and availability in uniform quality has made petroleum wax the standard for all candles. Only beeswax remains in use for religious candles where required.

As with many devices that man has developed, perfection of the candle to present-day quality and beauty took place over many centuries. Improvements have been step-wise, with the most significant advances having been made during recent years.

Indications are that candles will have an expanding economic future. Old crafts are being explored and extended in recognition of historical past and developed for present-day use.

With accumulated knowledge of petroleum wax and wicking, along with candle-production know-how, candles may be made to satisfy almost any appearance, burning time, and performance requirement. Candle possibilities are now limited only by the imagination. The following chapters were written to help that imagination toward producing a variety of candles.

2
Candles are Easy to Make

Candle making can be an enjoyable, practical hobby. The most difficult part of the art is not in making the candles but in seeing them be consumed when they burn.

Candles afford much pleasure as personalized gifts. The pleasure in the gift may be heightened by having that person in mind when the candle is made. Type of candle, style, and color preference are variations that may be utilized to please the receiver.

Anyone can make professional looking candles. There is however an analogy that should be kept in mind. Learning to make candles is like learning to run: you must first creep, then walk, and finally run as the tricks of the trade are learned. With practice and inventiveness the hobby may even become a new business.

A good place to start is in making a plain white molded candle. As in learning to run, the fancies will come later. Let us first consider the supplies that are needed for candle making. Better yet let us enumerate the items, and then consider them one by one.

1. A white general purpose paraffin wax should be obtained.
2. A safe means for melting and pouring the wax should be provided.
3. Convenient items for use as molds should be accumulated.
4. Proper wicking of correct type and size should be obtained to produce well-balanced candles that burn and perform well.

Paraffin wax is identified principally by melting point—the temperature at which the wax is converted from the solid state to the liquid state. A fully refined, white paraffin wax with a melting point of either 130–132° F. or 140–142° F. is to be preferred for general candle use. To obtain the wax, it is suggested that the

21

Candle Work Shop (Courtesy Candle Creations, Reading, Pa.)

sales office of a major petroleum refiner be contacted. The purpose for use of the wax should be stated. A local wax distributor may be suggested by the refiner and an identifying brand name may be given. For convenience, most refiners and distributors supply wax in ten-pound slabs, five to six slabs to a carton. Wax refiners and distributors, and their addresses, are listed in the Appendix.

Means for melting and handling the wax. Precautions should be observed in melting and handling paraffin wax. A work area should preferably be set aside for the purpose; a basement corner or an out-of-the-way spot in a garage may be convenient. If the kitchen must be used, it is suggested that surrounding surfaces be protected by a paper covering so that accidental spotting with melted wax may readily be cleaned up. Otherwise, spots and splashes

Candle Work Shop (Courtesy Candle Creations, Reading, Pa.)

are removed from surfaces by scraping with a dull putty knife or a spatula.

It is a safe practice to melt the wax in a metal container. A glass container should never be used, and the container should never be more than one third full. Remember wax will burn. Open flames are dangerous and splashes should be avoided. An old-fashioned enameled coffee pot with a pouring spout is a convenient utensil for melting the wax. A water-heated double boiler may also be used. By using water as the heat transfer medium, overheating is avoided. Water, however, should be kept out of the wax. Also, most double boilers have the disadvantage of not having a pouring spout. In this case a large tinned can with a pouring spout bent into one side of the rim may be used as a transfer pot from which to pour melted wax into the candle molds. These are suggestions; there are other suitable containers that may be used.

As a source of heat for melting the wax an electrical heating element is safer than an open gas flame. A thermostatically controlled hot plate or electrically heated deep fat fryer may also be used. For convenience in melting the wax it should be broken into suitable size pieces for placing into the melting container. A slab of wax may readily be broken into pieces by use of a hammer and a chisel. The slab may be cut into shavings by use of a butcher knife. (Cut down with the knife onto a wood surface.) Precautions should be taken that the wax be heated no hotter than 210° F. The 130 or the 140° F. melting point wax need be heated no hotter than 160 to 180° F. for pouring candles.

A convenient thermometer for checking the temperature of the melted wax is one that is an all-metal rod containing a bimetalic sensing element and having a dial scale at the top. These may be obtained in any laboratory supply house. With this type of thermometer, you may stir the wax while it is melting without fear of breakage. For uniformity in the candles the wax should be completely melted and stirred before it is poured into the molds. Further details on petroleum waxes are given in Chapter 4.

Let us now consider the candle mold. There are many household items that may be used as candle molds. Any container of suitable size with side walls that are slightly tapered outward is preferred. Containers with straight, smooth side walls may also be used. There should be no dents or ripples in the side wall if the solidified candle is to be conveniently removed. Obviously the container should be able to contain melted wax without leakage while the wax is solidifying.

Included among items that may be used as molds are: waxed-paper cups, an empty polyethylene-coated milk carton, an empty polyethylene-lined-fiber frozen-juice can, or a tinned can with smooth, undented side walls. An old-fashioned drink glass or similar glass having a heavy side wall and an outward taper may be used when it is preferred that the candle be burned in the mold. If need be, a candle molded in a glass of this type may also be removed to be burned as an unsupported candle. The outward taper of the side wall is helpful in releasing the candle from the glass mold.

Wicking is chosen to match the candle. A flat-plaited cotton wick is used where a hole may be pierced into the bottom of the mold. A metal-core wick is used in molds in which the wick must support itself, as for example in glass molds. Details on size selection and use are given further on in this discussion. Wicking is available in one-pound lots from the Atkins and Pearce Manufacturing Company (see Appendix). Some candle manufacturers may be willing to supply small quantities of candle wicking on special request.

Making the candle. Let us consider using a paper cup as an example of one type of candle mold and a glass tumbler as another.

When the paper cup is used, a small hole is punched into the center of the bottom, sufficiently large to allow threading the wick through the hole. Feed a suitable length of flat-plaited wick through the hole and arrange the wick as shown in Figure 4. The wick is threaded through the hole in the bottom of the cup with about one-half inch length folded against the bottom of the cup and fastened in place with a piece of adhesive tape, which also covers the hole. The length of wick within the cup is then carefully tied around a small bar or length of heavy gauge wire spanned across the open end of the cup. Care should be taken that the wick be centered and just barely taut without pulling out of the hole in the bottom. A 15-ply plaited wick is suggested for use in candles casted in eight-ounce or smaller cups. (With larger cups a 24-ply plaited wick is suggested.) These wicks may be used with either the 130 or the 140° F. melting point wax.

With the mold prepared, the wax is then readied for pouring into the mold where it is to be solidified to form a candle. A paper

FIGURE 4

PAPER CUP CANDLE MOLD

STEP ONE

HOLE CENTERED
IN BOTTOM OF
PAPER CUP.

STEP TWO

WICK THREADED THROUGH
HOLE AND COVERED ON
OUTSIDE OF BOTTOM WITH
ADHESIVE TAPE.

STEP THREE

TIE UPPER END OF WICK
TO WIRE BAR PLACED
ACROSS OPEN END OF
CUP WITH WICK
CENTERED IN CUP.

STEP FOUR

POUR MELTED WAX INTO CUP
AND ALLOW THE WAX TO SOLIDIFY.

STEP FIVE

STRIP PAPER CUP FROM SOLIDIFIED WAX
AND TRIM WICK FLUSH WITH LARGE DIAMETER
BASE OF THE CANDLE.

FIGURE 5

GLASS TUMBLER CANDLE MOLD

WICK TIN ENLARGED TO SHOW
STAR CUT STAMPED IN CENTER.

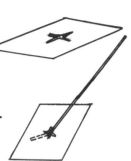

STEP ONE

PLACE END OF METAL CORE WICK
THROUGH STAR CUT IN WICK TIN
AND BEND TIPS OF STAR DOWN
TO HOLD WICK IN PLACE.

STEP TWO

PLACE WICK TIN and WICK
IN TUMBLER WITH WICK
CENTERED BY LOOP IN WIRE ROD
PLACED ACROSS TOP OF TUMBLER.

STEP THREE

POUR WAX and ALLOW WAX
TO SOLIDIFY. A CONICAL
CAVITY MAY FORM ON TOP
SURFACE AROUND THE WICK.

STEP FOUR

MAKE SECOND POUR OF WAX
TO FILL CAVITY AND PROVIDE
A LEVEL SURFACE TO THE CANDLE.

NOTE – CANDLE MAY BE BURNED IN TUMBLER
OR IT MAY BE REMOVED BY TAPPING
TO REUSE TUMBLER AS A MOLD.

cup mold should best be standing on a cold surface or in a shallow depth of ice water. This is to aid solidification and prevent leakage of melted wax from the cup. Wax-pouring temperature is suggested to be no hotter than about 20° F. above its melting point, or at most 180° F. with the 130 or 140° F. melting point waxes. Excess heat only prolongs the time for solidification of the wax. When the wax in the cup is completely solidified, the paper is stripped from the candle and the wick is removed from the supporting rod and trimmed flush to the candle surface. Note that the top of the candle in the mold becomes the bottom of the self-supported candle when it is burned.

When a glass tumbler or jar is used as a mold, a metal core wick is used as shown in Figure 5. The bottom end of the metal-core wick is crimped into a thin metal plate and placed into the center of the jar. The metal core allows the wick to support itself in the glass while the wax is poured and solidified. The wick-holding device supported on the top of the jar holds the wick centered in the jar or glass. A 34–20 metal-core wick is suggested for use with the 132° F. melting point wax in candles up to two and one half inches in diameter. If a larger diameter glass or a higher melting point wax is used, a 36–24–24 metal-core wick is suggested for the candle to obtain best performance.

Pouring and solidification of the wax in the glass mold is performed essentially the same as with the paper cup mold with one exception: the top of the candle in the mold is the top of the candle when it is burned in the glass. As such, if there is a concavity in the top surface of the solidified candle this cavity should be filled in with melted wax to provide a smooth level surface. The wick support at the top of the glass is then removed and cut to a one-half inch length above the surface of the candle.

If a tapered glass jar is used as a mold, and when the wax is completely solidified, the candle may be removed by sharply tapping the open end of the jar on a table top. If tapping does not readily release it from the jar, chilling the jar and candle in a refrigerator will help to shrink the candle from the jar wall and aid release.

Two types of candles have been described. With originality a great variety of artistic and novel candles may be made. Many forms and types of materials may be used as molds including metals, plastics, plasters, and flexible rubbers. All are discussed in detail in later sections of this book.

In summary, while candle making can be fun, there are precautions that should be observed and are repeated here for emphasis.

1. Never over heat candle wax. It will burn if heated to excessively high temperatures. Heating wax to 20° F. above its melting point is sufficiently hot enough for pouring and is quite safe.

2. Avoid splashes of hot wax. If it splashes onto the skin, immediately place the affected part under cold running water and then carefully remove the solidified wax.

3. To clean utensils of wax, pour the major portion of melted wax into a storage can, then wipe the wax from the utensil with a cloth or paper towels while it is still melted.

4. Do not pour melted wax or hot water containing wax down a drain. Upon solidification, wax will clog a sanitary drain.

5. Use only wax soluble dyes to color candle wax. (See the section on additives discussed in Chapter 6.) Pigments as used in crayons are not soluble in candle wax and should not be used. Pigment settles from the wax, and if it is in the candle when burned, it will plug the wick and degrade its performance.

3
Science in a Candle?

This chapter is intended to point out briefly that there is general science, chemistry, and physics involved in candle making and candle burning. It is written for general interest and is addressed principally to the candle hobbyist, with some sidelights for the commercial candle manufacturer. A cursory look at the scientific background to candles is included for completeness.

The question may be asked, "Of what use is a candle if it does not burn well and perform properly?" Over the years this question has been asked many times as inferior candles were made for use. It has been through scientific inquiry that answers have been obtained toward improving products, including the candle. Answers have come in stepwise improvements.

As with many simple devices, the candle was not always the precise product made available for use today. Original candles burned poorly, smoked excessively, and dripped unburned wax, and some had an offensive odor. With application of practical knowledge and scientific principles the candle was improved in time to its present-day level of high quality. Excellent appearance and performance may now be built into candles through choice of wax and wick along with manufacturing control in producing a wide variety of candles.

It was previously stated in elementary terms that a candle is made of a solidified fuel surrounding a wick. It is quite apparent that the fuel must not only be solid at ordinary temperature, it must also be solid at rather high temperature storage conditions. In addition, the fuel must liquefy at flame temperature in sufficient quantity to adequately feed the flame when the candle is burned. Also, the liquefied fuel must readily wick up to the flame by capillarity, where it must then vaporize properly to burn with a soot-free flame. These factors may seem to be commonplace and may be taken for granted. They are, however, achieved only if the candle fuel has been carefully chosen. It must have the correct melting point and proper volatility, as well as excellent combustibility. Though not generally thought of, neither the solid state nor the liquid state of the fuel is burned in the candle. It is the vapor state that is burned at flame temperature. Through research there now are specially refined petroleum waxes that provide the properties required of a high grade candle wax.

Involved chemical and physical detail on atomic structure, rates of reaction, and thermodynamics of combustion are outside the intent of this discussion. These are involved subjects on which standard texts and reference books have been written and to which the reader is referred if interested (see references). To provide a general understanding of the science involved in a candle only elementary chemistry and physics need be presented for general comprehension.

It is basic that all matter, including candle wax, is made up of atoms. An atom may be defined as the smallest part of a chemical element that retains the identity of that element. For example carbon, hydrogen, and oxygen are chemical elements. These elements abound in nature and are basic in a discussion on use and combustion of candle wax.

When atoms combine, molecules are formed. For example, when atoms of carbon and hydrogen are in combination the molecules of matter are known as hydrocarbons. Petroleum wax is a mixture of hydrocarbons known as paraffins. The term paraffin indicates that the carbon atoms in the hydrocarbon are fully saturated with hydrogen. In chemical notation, petroleum wax hydrocarbons range from $C_{20}H_{42}$ up to about $C_{40}H_{82}$. Note that there are twice as many hydrogen atoms plus 2 as there are carbon atoms in a paraffin hydrocarbon molecule. This is characteristic of a paraffin.

Oxygen is a very important and fortunately very common chemical element in nature. It supports normal combustion, and most living matter is dependent upon its presence for existence. At normal conditions of temperature and pressure oxygen is a gaseous component of the earth's atmosphere.

Combustion is a rapid oxidation process. When the hydrocarbons in a candle wax are burned in an excess of air, the carbon atoms combine with oxygen atoms to form carbon dioxide, while the hydrogen atoms are burned to form water. This can be shown in chemical notation by selecting the simple hydrocarbon, methane, which has the structural formula CH_4. A balanced equation showing complete burning of methane is written as follows:

$$CH_4 + 2O_2 \longrightarrow CO_2 + 2H_2O + HEAT$$

With heat being generated, this reaction is said to be exothermic. At flame temperature and normal atmospheric pressure both water and carbon dioxide are gaseous products and thus are not seen, only light may be seen and heat may be felt as evidence of combustion.

With this brief discussion on combustion, past and present candle fuels may now be considered. As previously pointed out in Chapter 1, solid animal fats and natural waxes were originally used as candle fuels. While they may now be provided in a highly refined state, or made synthetically, they are far too expensive for candle use in comparison to paraffin wax. In addition, no one fat or natural wax is satisfactory in all respects for candle use.

For completeness of discussion it may be of interest to consider the chemistry of fats and natural waxes, which surprisingly enough are chemically related. Animals produce fats, while some insects and some plants produce natural waxes. They are comprised of molecules that contain carbon, hydrogen, and oxygen. As such they belong to a class of chemical compounds known as esters. Animal fats are glyceryl esters of fatty acids. Insect and plant waxes contain esters of high molecular weight alcohols combined with an organic acid. Stearin is an example of an animal fat, beeswax an example of an insect wax, and carnauba wax an example of a plant wax. All have been used in producing candles.

Fats and natural waxes being esters are formed when an alcohol is chemically reacted with an organic acid. This reaction takes place through the hydroxyl of the alcohol and the carboxyl group of the organic acid. In greater detail for explanation, an alcohol is a carbon-hydrogen molecule containing an —OH group, known as a hydroxyl group. An organic acid is a carbon-hydrogen molecule containing a $-C\overset{\displaystyle O}{\underset{\displaystyle OH}{\big<}}$ group, known as a carboxyl group. If R is used to designate the carbon-hydrogen portion of the molecule, ester formation may be represented by the following chemical equation.

$$\text{R.C}\!\!\begin{array}{c}\nearrow^{O}\\\searrow_{OH}\end{array} + \text{R,OH} \longrightarrow \text{R,O} \!\!\begin{array}{c}\searrow\\\nearrow\end{array}\!\! C\!-\!R + H_2O$$

   (Acid)   (Alcohol)   (Ester) (Water)

For example, a beeswax component results from reaction of Myricyl alcohol ($C_{30}H_{61}$—OH) with Palmitic acid ($C_{15}H_{31}COOH$) to form Myricyl Palmitate. It is to be noted that in natural waxes, the alcohol part of the molecule contains but one —OH group.

In fats, however, the alcohol is always glycerine, which contains three —OH groups. Stearin, for example, as a component of beef fat, is the reaction product of glycerine ($C_3H_5(OH)_3$) and stearic acid ($C_{17}H_{35}COOH$). In stearin all three —OH groups of the glycerine molecule are replaced with the stearic acid radical. In nomenclature to designate this, the product is classified as a tri-glyceride, known chemically as glyceryl tri-stearate. Thus:

$$C_3H_5(OH)_3 + 3C_{17}H_{35}COOH \longrightarrow C_3H_5(OC\!\!\begin{array}{c}\nearrow^{O}\\\searrow_{C_{17}H_{35}}\end{array}\!\!)_3$$

  (Glycerine)   (Stearic Acid)   (Glyceryl Tri-Stearate)

Both fats and natural waxes contain fatty acids combined in their molecule. A fatty acid is defined as an organic acid in which there is a chain of at least six carbon atoms, and containing only one carboxyl group in the molecule. As can readily be seen, any one of a great variety of fatty acids may react with the tri-hydric alcohol (glycerine) to form a fat. With all three hydroxyl groups of the glycerine molecule replaced with a fatty acid molecule, that particular variety of fat is produced. With the great number of possible fatty acids, it may thus be seen that the difference among fats is due to the size (molecular weight) of the fatty acid component. With natural waxes the difference among them is due both to the size of the alcohol molecule, as well as to the size of the fatty acid molecule.

While nature provides only even carbon-number fatty acids, man may synthesize a variety of uneven carbon number fatty acids. Thus it is seen that a great number of natural and synthetic fats or "natural type" waxes are possible for candle use. However, none can compete with paraffin wax on cost or performance basis.

Well now, what about the natural fats and waxes that were used in making original candles? The fat or wax had to be solid at room temperature and preferably melt above about 120° F. Several representative fats and waxes are given in the following table to illustrate the fact that these materials are solid at room temperature, and that there is a melting point increase with increase in molecular weight within each type compound. (See Table No. 1.)

Table No. 1

Chemical Name	Type Compound	Carbon No. Alcohol	Carbon No. Acid	Mol. Wt.	M.P.°F
Glyceryl Laurate	Fat	$C_3H_5 (OH)_3$ (Glycerine)	C_{12}	638.58	115.5
Glyceryl Myristate	Fat	(Glycerine)	C_{14}	722.67	134.6
Glyceryl Palmitate	Fat	(Glycerine)	C_{16}	806.76	149.9
Glyceryl Stearate	Fat	(Glycerine)	C_{18}	890.96	160.7
Stearyl Myristate	Wax	$C_{18}H_{37} (OH)$	C_{14}	466.51	125.6
Ceryl Myristate	Wax	$C_{26}H_{53} (OH)$	C_{14}	652.64	143.6
Myricyl Palmitate	Wax	$C_{14}H_{29} (OH)$	C_{16}	452.48	161.6
Myricyl Stearate	Wax	$C_{14}H_{29} (OH)$	C_{18}	480.51	168.8

Nature being complex in her ways, fats and waxes were found by analysis to be complex mixtures of related compounds, rather than single compounds. Being mixtures the melting point was lowered. Thus, crude mixtures were refined to isolate components and raise melting point. Simple but nevertheless practical procedures were used to refine these mixtures. For example, boiling water treatment was employed. Refined fat or wax was skimmed from the surface of the water and foreign unwanted matter was either dissolved by the water or settled to the bottom. In this way a practical separation was made.

As chemical reactions were explored, refining of fats and waxes by chemical means came to be practiced. For example, wood ashes, which contain an alkali potassium carbonate, were used to split a fat into glycerine and form a potassium soap of the fatty acid. This came to be known in the trade as fat splitting or saponification. The process may be represented as follows:

Fat + Alkali $\longrightarrow$ Glycerine + Soap

Without going into details, the wood ashes were steeped in boiling water to dissolve the alkali. The fat was added to the boiling alkaline water to split out glycerine that dissolved in the water. The soap that formed was concentrated by boiling off most of the water. Soap concentrate was then skimmed from the surface of the water and recovered for use. The soap may then have been split with mineral acid in a second operation to release the fatty acid.

With beef fat stearin (glyceryl stearate), this series of operations may be summarized as follows:

(1) Glyceryl Stearate + Potassium hydroxide ⟶
      (Stearin, a fat)   (alkali)
      Potassium Stearate + Glycerine
          (soap)
(2) Potassium Stearate + Hydrochloric Acid ⟶
          (soap)   (Mineral Acid)
      Stearic Acid + Potassium Chloride

Refined stearin and stearic acid released from the fat were among second-generation candle fuels. Refined stearic acid was effectively used to harden soft fats and soft paraffin wax. It is too hard and brittle to be used alone.

As might be guessed from the above discussion, in Colonial times soaps and candles were part of the same craft or trade. The merchant in this trade came to be known as a chandler, designating one who dealt in candles and soap.

Discovery of "Rock Oil," petroleum as it is known today (*petro* meaning rock, *oleum* meaning oil), was destined to greatly influence the candle industry. Crude petroleum oil was found to contain paraffin wax. The marvel is that a white wax may be refined from a black crude oil. With the development of petroleum refining techniques paraffin wax was isolated from wax bearing fractions. By refining the crude paraffin wax to a white product, natural fats and waxes were displaced for candle use. Increased availability of refined paraffin wax contributed directly to the expansion of the candle industry. To further contribute to it, custom-made grades of petroleum wax were then made available for use in the many types and varieties of candles that came to be developed.

Physical properties have been used as guides for specific use of the grades of paraffin wax. Among these properties melting point is most important. Other important properties include melting point range, boiling range, hardness, change in hardness with temperature, viscosity, oil content, burning point or flash point temperature, contraction on solidification, and brittleness. Any or all of these properties may be used to define the paraffin wax most suitable for use in producing a particular candle wax. Chemistry and technology of petroleum wax refining is the subject of the following chapter.

4
Chemistry and Technology
of Petroleum Wax

Petroleum wax is the fuel used in most present-day candles. This chapter on the chemistry and technology of petroleum wax is presented so that the candle maker may have an insight into the variety of petroleum waxes that is available for use. Petroleum wax, a mixture of rather crystalline hydrocarbons, is physically separated from distillation fractions of wax-bearing crude oil. Refining procedures, especially for wax production, are briefly described in this chapter.

There are many types of crude oil, all of which are mixtures of hydrocarbons. Some are entirely gaseous, others are entirely asphaltic. Between these two extremes there are complete crudes that contain a full range of primary petroleum products. In refining a complete crude oil, it is first separated by distillation into fractions, known sometimes as cuts. Each cut is made with a predetermined boiling range. These cuts include hydrocarbon gas, straight run gasoline, fuel oil distillate, light lube oil cuts, heavy lube oil cuts, and pipe still bottoms, in order of increased boiling point. Each cut covers a boiling range of hydrocarbon components.

The pipe still is a continuous distillation unit comprising a tower within which there is a number of bubble-cap trays arranged in tiers. In operation, crude oil is pumped through a coiled pipe in a furnace to heat the oil and increase the vapor pressure of its components. The heated crude oil is then introduced into the fractionation tower part way up the side. The most volatile components work their way up to the top of the tower, while the least volatile components work their way down to the bottom. Fractionation is

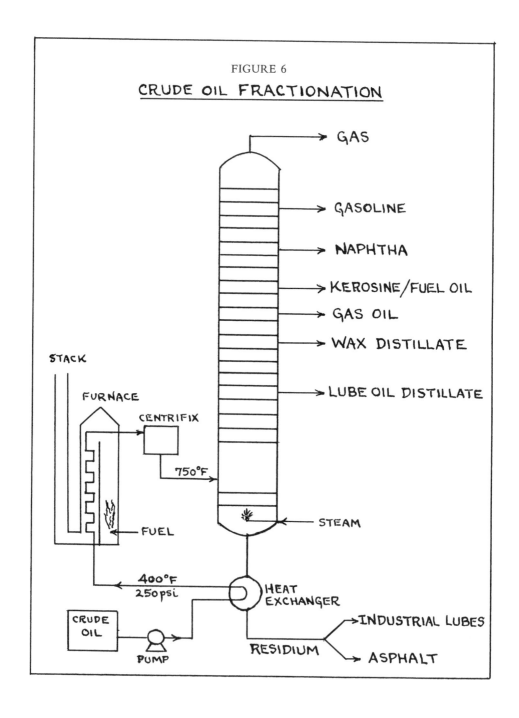

FIGURE 6

CRUDE OIL FRACTIONATION

thereby accomplished. Cuts are taken from the tower as pipe still streams; each one is then stored separately in tankage for further processing. This is shown diagrammatically in Figure 6.

In wax-bearing crudes, wax is present in the light and heavy lube oil cuts, as well as in the pipe still bottoms. During early days of petroleum refining, wax present in light lube oil distillates was removed by chilling the distillate and filtering out the wax. Oil occluded in the filter cake was then removed in an operation that was known as sweating. This operation was dependent upon the needle-like structure of the wax that was obtained after the filtered wax was melted and then slowly resolidified. This wax, known in the trade as slack wax, in some cases contained as much as 20 per cent oil. The needle structure of the resolidified wax allowed the oil to drain from the wax.

In performing the sweating operation the slack wax was melted and charged to pans or trays arranged in tiers in a large room. Each tray contained a wire mesh screen several inches from the bottom of the tray. Water was charged to each tray to a level just above the screen. Melted slack wax was floated on the water, whereupon the room was cooled to solidify the wax. When the wax was completely solidified the water was drained from the pans, bringing the solidified wax down onto the screens. The temperature in the room was then slowly raised, which allowed occluded oil and low-melting wax components to "sweat" from the cake. The low-melting wax and oil was drained away leaving an oil-free "sweated wax" on the screen in the pans. The sweated wax was then melted from the pans, sulfuric acid treated in the melted state, caustic neutralized, then clay filtered to produce a white, finished paraffin wax. A schematic diagram of this operation is shown in Figure 7.

Unfortunately the crystal structure of the wax in chilled high boiling distillates and pipe still bottoms did not allow refining by the sweating operation. The very small or "microcrystalline" structure of wax present in high-boiling fractions holds onto oil like a sponge. To recover wax from these fractions solvent dilution was found to be effective. In the solvent refining process, the wax-bearing fraction is taken up in a mixed solvent.

One part of the solvent dissolves the oil, the other part precipitates the wax. A mixture of benzene and toluene is used as the oil solvent, while methyl-ethyl ketone is used as the wax precipitant. The composition or ratio of the components in the mixed solvent is adjusted to the waxy stock being processed. The solvent is then

FIGURE 7

WAX SWEATING OPERATION

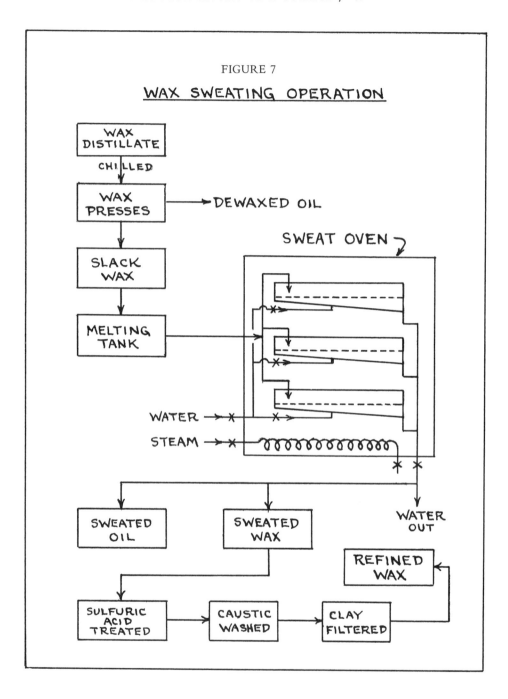

adjusted to the waxy stock (in stock to solvent ratio) to obtain fluidity of the oil solution for filtration, and to obtain a filter cake of oil-free wax. In this operation the mixed solvent and the de-waxing stock are warmed together to obtain a complete solution. The mix is then chilled to a predetermined temperature, to sepa-rate the wax that is to be filtered. A rotary drum filter is most often used, in which case the drum covered with filter cloth and under vacuum rotates on a horizontal axis partially submerged in the wax slurry. Dewaxed oil and solvent are pulled through the filter and drained into filtrate receivers. Wax cake builds up on the filter cloth. It is washed with solvent spray, suction dried, then blown from the filter. For further purification the wax cake may be taken up in additional solvent and put through a second filtration. The first filtrate may also be lowered in temperature to recover lower melting "filtrate wax." The solvent is then removed from the wax and oil fractions by distillation. The wax may then be refined by hydrogenation to produce a white, low-oil content finished wax. This solvent process for wax refining is so versatile that modern petroleum wax refiners now employ this process for their entire wax production. A summary flow diagram of the solvent refining operation is given in Figure 8.

With this brief discussion on wax refining, let us now consider the chemical structure and physical properties of paraffin waxes as isolated from the several petroleum fractions. To begin with, the carbon atoms in a paraffin wax are attached together as in a back-bone or skeletal structure. All carbon atoms in a paraffin wax molecule are fully saturated with hydrogen. Structurally there are three classes or types of paraffins: normal, iso-paraffins, and cyclo-paraffins. Assuming a 15-carbon atom molecule, these structures are shown as follows:

C_{15} *Normal Paraffin,* $C_{15}H_{32}$ could be written:

$$H-\underset{\displaystyle H}{\overset{\displaystyle H}{C}}-\underset{\displaystyle H}{\overset{\displaystyle H}{C}}-\underset{\displaystyle H}{\overset{\displaystyle H}{C}}-\underset{\displaystyle H}{\overset{\displaystyle H}{C}}-\underset{\displaystyle H}{\overset{\displaystyle H}{C}}-\underset{\displaystyle H}{\overset{\displaystyle H}{C}}-\underset{\displaystyle H}{\overset{\displaystyle H}{C}}-\underset{\displaystyle H}{\overset{\displaystyle H}{C}}-\underset{\displaystyle H}{\overset{\displaystyle H}{C}}-\underset{\displaystyle H}{\overset{\displaystyle H}{C}}-\underset{\displaystyle H}{\overset{\displaystyle H}{C}}-\underset{\displaystyle H}{\overset{\displaystyle H}{C}}-\underset{\displaystyle H}{\overset{\displaystyle H}{C}}-\underset{\displaystyle H}{\overset{\displaystyle H}{C}}-\underset{\displaystyle H}{\overset{\displaystyle H}{C}}-H$$

Note that there are no side chains present; all of the carbons are in one chain.

C_{15} *Iso-Paraffin,* $C_{15}H_{32}$ one of many possibilities could be:

Note the presence of side chains in this molecule.

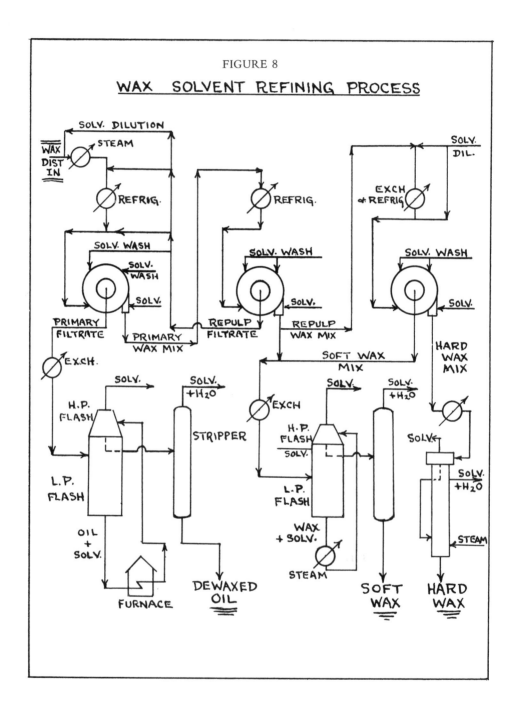

FIGURE 8

WAX SOLVENT REFINING PROCESS

C_{15} *Cyclo-Paraffin,* $C_{15}H_{32}$ also with many possible arrangements, one of which could be:

$$\begin{array}{c}
\text{CH}_2 \\
\end{array}$$

H₂C   CH–C–C–C–C–C–C–C–C–CH₃

H₂C——CH₂

Note the five carbon atom cyclic group to which a side chain is attached.

Paraffins in the lower melting petroleum waxes are predominantly normal in structure as isolated from most wax-bearing crude oils. Iso-paraffins are present principally in the higher melting petroleum waxes, in concentrations dependent upon crude source.

It is to be noted that all three types of C_{15} paraffins have a condensed formula of $C_{15}H_{32}$. This condensed formula gives a clue to the empirical formula for all paraffins, which is C_nH_{2n+2}. Thus, all paraffins contain twice as many hydrogen atoms plus 2 more in comparison to the number of carbon atoms in the molecule. With this brief background to paraffin wax chemistry, let us now consider the more important physical properties of paraffin wax as related to candle making.

Physical properties of a paraffin wax, as will be seen, are related to the arrangement and number of carbon atoms in the molecule. In candle making, melting point, hardness, and viscosity of a wax are among its more important physical properties. That these properties vary with the paraffin chemical structure, and the number of carbon atoms in the molecule, is shown using melting point in the following example:

Paraffin Hydrocarbon	Approximate[1] Melting Point, °F.
Normal–$C_{28}H_{58}$	143
Iso–$C_{28}H_{58}$	112
Normal–$C_{29}H_{60}$	147
Iso–$C_{29}H_{60}$	118
Normal–$C_{30}H_{62}$	151
Iso–$C_{30}H_{62}$	124

[1] Indications are that iso-paraffin hydrocarbons have a melting point that is about the same as the normal paraffin having six less carbon atoms in the molecule.

Thus, for a given boiling point or carbon number wax, normal paraffins melt at a higher temperature and are harder at a given temperature than are the corresponding iso- or cyclo-paraffins.

The melting point example for pure paraffin hydrocarbons was given for simplicity. Petroleum wax as produced is not a pure compound, but rather a mixture of the paraffin type hydrocarbons, as previously indicated. A typical 130° F. melting point paraffin wax obtained from a light lube oil distillate is an example. It may contain 95 per cent normal paraffins in combination with 5 per cent iso-paraffins, and these paraffins may have a carbon number range from C_{20} to C_{35}. The crude oil from which this wax was obtained may contain paraffins from C_{15} to about C_{100}, distributed over the entire wax bearing-portion of the crude.

It is now becoming obvious that wax characteristics may be modified and controlled by adjusting refining operations to produce a wide variety of paraffin waxes. Pipe stilling is the primary operation, in which separation takes place by boiling-point range. Solvent refining the distillation cuts is the secondary operation, in which separation is effected by melting-point range. To reduce the carbon number distribution of the wax contained in a distillation cut, the boiling range of the cut is narrowed. The carbon number distribution in the recovered wax may be further narrowed in the solvent refining process. By increasing the solvent content in the stock to solvent mix, and by conducting the filtration at a relatively high temperature, the carbon number distribution is narrowed. To broaden the carbon number distribution, a lower filtration temperature is employed, with the solvent content adjusted for ease of filtration. Paraffin types in the wax composition may also be controlled in the solvent process. In general, as the carbon number distribution is broadened in a wax, by adjusting the solvent process, there is an increase in the iso- and cyclo-paraffin content of the finished wax. In this way lower melting iso- and cyclo-paraffins are included along with the higher melting normal paraffins. The presence of iso- and cyclo-paraffins soften and make the wax more plastic. Thus wax isolated from a given crude may have a preselected melting point, melting-point range, boiling range, and paraffin-type composition. All of these variations influence the handling and performance characteristics of the wax when used to make candles.

The principles of petroleum wax refining described may be illustrated graphically as follows:

    1. *Fractionation of wax-bearing crude oil* (See Figure 9)
        (a) Primary fractionation by boiling range (distillation)
        (b) Secondary fractionation by melting-point range (solvent refining) .
    2. *Distillation cuts may be broad or narrow*[2] (See Figure 10)

------

[2]*Note* that both broad and narrow cut materials have the same 50 per cent point.

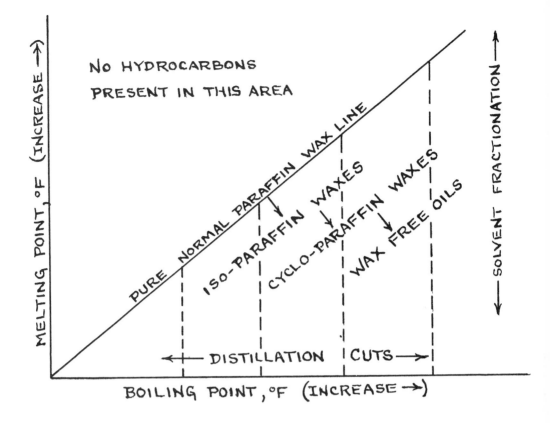

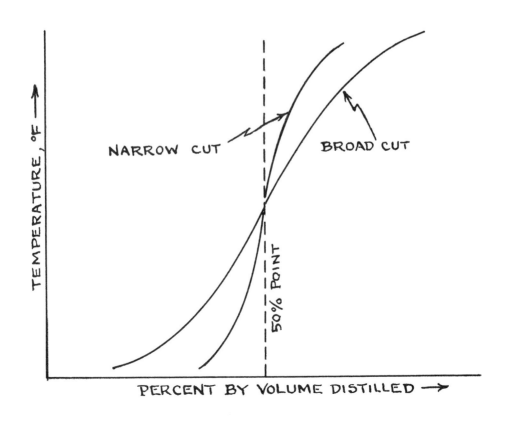

3. *Wax melting point distribution may be* (See Figure 11)
   (a) Broad or narrow, with same average M.P.[3]

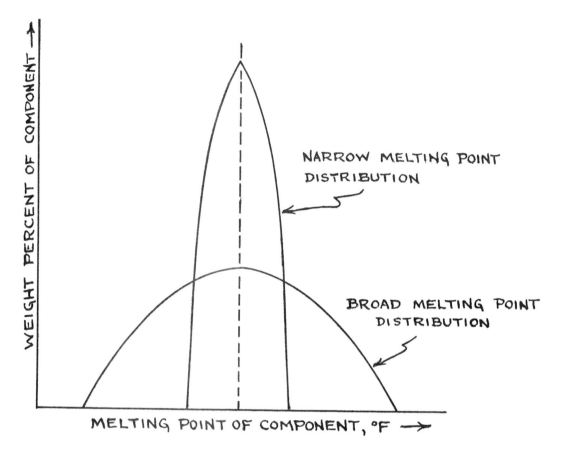

FIGURE 11

   (b) Skewed or evenly distributed wax with same average M.P. See Figure 12, page 47.
   (c) An overlapping wax blend, with same average M.P. See Figure 13, page 48.

These graphs show that in a paraffin wax having a given determined melting point, the boiling range, melting-point range, and paraffin type composition may be varied initially by refining and secondarily by wax blending. With this variability in paraffin wax

---

[3] *Note* that while both waxes may have the same average melting point, they will be different in other physical properties for candle making.

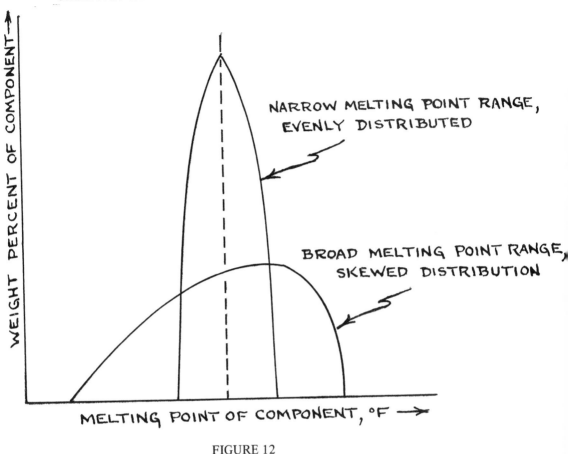

FIGURE 12

composition being possible, it can readily be seen that a paraffin wax may be custom made for a given candle production process, or to achieve given performance properties.

There are three basic factors involved in selecting a paraffin wax for best performance in a candle production procedure and for appearance, as well as burning quality. These factors are:

1. The melting point must be judiciously selected.
2. The melting point distribution of components in the wax must be selected or adjusted for the candle performance desired.
3. The relative distribution of paraffin types in the wax, i.e. normal paraffins, iso-paraffins, and cyclo-paraffins, must be

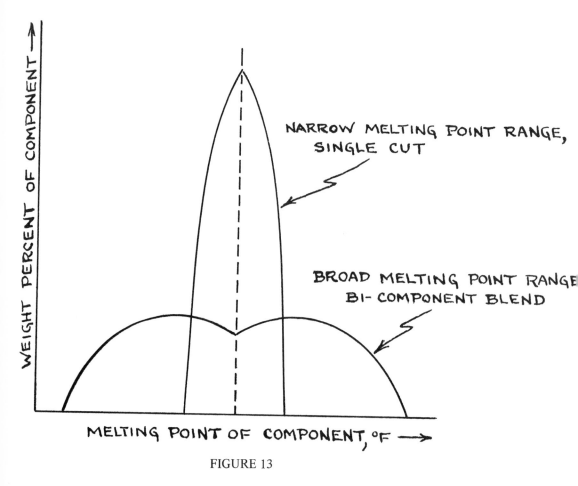

WEIGHT PERCENT OF COMPONENT →

NARROW MELTING POINT RANGE, SINGLE CUT

BROAD MELTING POINT RANGE BI- COMPONENT BLEND

MELTING POINT OF COMPONENT, °F →

FIGURE 13

adjusted for best handling in production and best performance in the candle.

Wax selection and formulation is discussed in the chapters on production of specific type candles. There are, however, certain generalities on wax properties that may be considered in the remaining part of this chapter.

That paraffin wax composition influences wax properties in candle use may be shown by considering the pertinent properties one at a time.

1. *Melting Point* (There are three procedures that may be used to determine melting point.)

    (a) *By Cooling Curve* A.S.T.M. Method D-87

        By definition this method measures the temperature at

which melted paraffin wax first shows a minimum rate of temperature change when allowed to cool under prescribed conditions. It is the temperature at which the melted wax evolves the heat that was absorbed when it was being melted. It is measured as a rate of cooling under standardized conditions.

A sharp, long, cooling curve flat, in which the wax temperature remains the same over a long period of time, generally indicates the wax to be close cut, with a high normal paraffin content. By broadening the wax-melting point distribution, or by making it more non-normal, the melting point flat is shortened. In extreme, a very broad melting range, highly non-normal petroleum wax has no cooling curve flat. A typical cooling curve for each of the several types of paraffin wax is shown in the following graph:

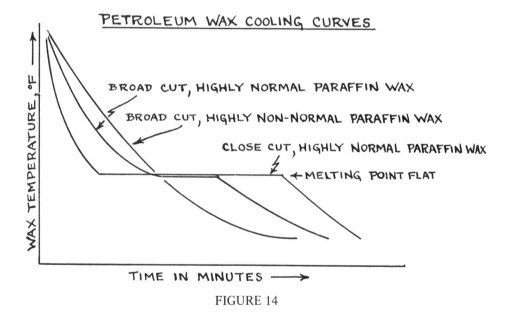

FIGURE 14

(b) *"Drop" Melting Point* A.S.T.M. Method D-127

By definition this method measures the temperature at which a thin film of solidified wax on the bulb of a thermometer becomes sufficiently fluid to drop from the bulb when warmed under prescribed conditions. This method is used with waxes that have no cooling curve flat, including petrolatums and microwaxes that are high in iso-paraffinic content.

(c) *Congealing Point*   A.S.T.M. Method D-938

Congealing point is that temperature at which a film of melted wax or petrolatum coating the bulb of a thermometer ceases to flow when cooled under prescribed conditions, while the thermometer is slowly rotated in a horizontal plane.

Melting point characteristics, along with other properties of a paraffin wax to be described are useful in predicting performance of a candle wax. These properties are further discussed in chapters on specific type candles.

2. *Change in Hardness with Increase in Temperature*   A.S.T.M. Method D-1321

Hardness of a paraffin wax is measured as depth of needle penetration (in 0.1 millimeter) into a block of the wax at test temperature under a 100-gram load during five seconds time. Test temperatures are 77°, 100°, and 120° F. to measure change in hardness with increase in temperature. Rate of change in hardness is significant in wax for candle use.

A close-cut, highly normal paraffin wax will usually retain considerable hardness until it reaches a temperature where sudden softening takes place. A broad cut, highly non-normal paraffin wax will exhibit greater softening as temperature is increased. This is illustrated in Figures 15 and 16:

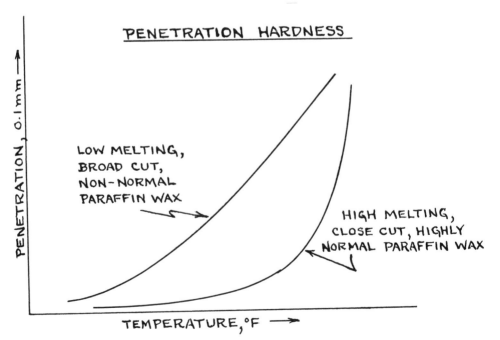

FIGURE 15

It should be noted that while the two types of wax may have the same melting point, they will handle differently in candle production and the candle will perform differently when burned. Once again these differences are best discussed in following chapters on production and performance of specific type candles. The influence of temperature upon hardness of selected candle waxes is shown in Figure 16. Other properties of these waxes are given in Table No. 2.

3. *Transition temperature*

The transition temperature of a wax is that temperature at which it undergoes a crystallographic change in cooling from the liquid to the completely solid state. At this temperature the wax converts from a plastic non-crystalline form to a crystalline one. The temperature at which the transition takes place is usually 25 to 30° F. below the melting point of the wax. It is seen as a second flat in a continuation of the cooling curve by the D-87 test method. It may be seen as a second peak in determining coefficient of expansion as temperature is lowered. The first peak in expansion occurs at the melting point; the second peak occurs

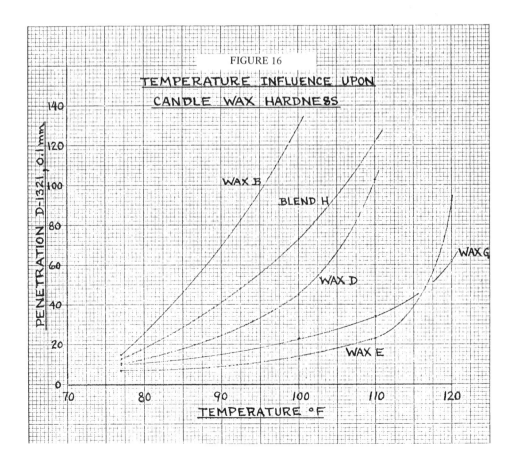

FIGURE 16

TEMPERATURE INFLUENCE UPON CANDLE WAX HARDNESS

at the transition temperature. The transition temperature may also be seen in reverse as the temperature at which there is a sudden decrease in hardness when the temperature of the paraffin wax is raised.

As a generality, a highly normal close-cut paraffin wax will exhibit a sharp transition temperature. Below this temperature it will be crystalline, hard, and brittle. As iso-paraffinic content of the wax is increased and the melting-point range is broadened, the transition temperature of the wax becomes less apparent. In extreme there is no transition temperature. A highly iso-paraffinic wax does not go into the crystalline state upon solidification. It is amorphous, and being rather non-crystalline in the solid state it is usually plastic over the entire solid temperature range.

Wax characteristics play a part in candle performance. A rigid, but not brittle, hard wax is required for self-supporting molded candles. Large diameter candles that are to form petals of unburned wax must have a degree of plasticity. Candles produced by extrusion or compression of chipped or powdered wax must have the right amount of plasticity at candle-forming temperature.

Thus the degree to which a transition temperature exists indicates handling characteristics of the wax in candle production, and candle performance characteristics when stored for use and when burned. A candle will sag in a holder or will soften out of shape and adhere to other candles in a box if exposed to temperatures above the transition point. For these reasons it can be seen that it is important to select a wax with the correct melting point, since if a transition point is present it is related to the melting point. It becomes apparent that the extent and temperature of transition in a paraffin wax determines the suitability of the wax for use in a given type of candle.

4. *Change in viscosity with increase in temperature* A.S.T.M.
Method D-445

This method covers the determination of kinematic viscosity of a liquid, including fully melted paraffin wax. Determinations may be made at any temperature where the flow in a glass capillary-tube viscometer is Newtonian. In Newtonian flow the rate of shear is proportional to the shearing stress. By definition then, constant ratio of shearing stress to rate of shear is the viscosity of the liquid.

A close-cut, highly normal paraffin wax has a lower viscosity

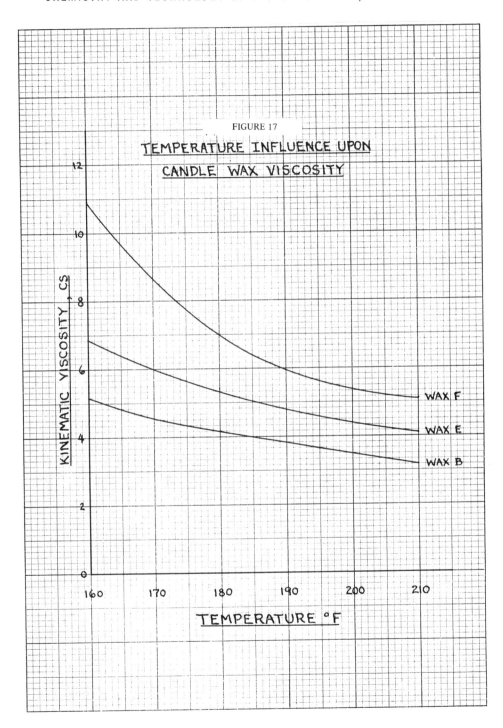

FIGURE 17

TEMPERATURE INFLUENCE UPON

CANDLE WAX VISCOSITY

than a broad-cut, highly non-normal wax with the same melting point. In general, the viscosity of the close-cut wax changes less with increase in temperature than does the broad cut. Also, viscosity of a wax increases with increase in wax melting point. The influence of temperature upon viscosity of selected candle waxes is shown in Figure 17. Other properties of these waxes are given in Table 2 and Table 20.

Viscosity has an important influence upon burning rate of a given candle wax when a given wick is used. The higher the viscosity, the lower the rate of capillarity, with consequent lower burning rate of the candle.

5. *Oil content*   A.S.T.M. Method D-721

Oil is distinguished from paraffin wax as that component of the wax which is liquid at room temperature. As was pointed out in the discussion of sweating, some waxes release oil more readily than others. A highly normal paraffin wax, with a rather large plate structure, releases occluded oil more easily than does a highly non-normal wax with a rather small needle structure. Small needle structured wax, sometimes referred to as a micro-wax, tends to retain oil somewhat as a sponge retains water.

A solvent procedure is employed to accommodate the several types of petroleum wax for oil determination. In this method the wax sample is dissolved in methyl-ethyl ketone and cooled to $-25°$ F. to precipitate the wax. The solution is filtered and the oil content of the filtrate is determined by evaporating the methyl-ethyl ketone and weighing the residue. Oil content is calculated as weight percent of the wax sample taken.

Depending upon the paraffin type, a petroleum wax with a 10 to 20 percent oil content may be more or less mushy. A high-melting, iso-paraffinic microwax could retain this oil, while a lower-melting, highly normal paraffin wax will be mushy. Even a moderate oil content of 2 to 5 percent in a highly normal paraffin wax will destroy a firm and good-appearing wax structure. For best performance in a self-supported candle, a fully refined paraffin wax with an oil content no higher than 0.5 percent is preferred. Candles cast and burned in jars may be made with a paraffin wax containing as much as 1.5 percent oil without degrading performance.

6. *Flash point*   A.S.T.M. Method D-92

The flash point of a petroleum wax is defined as the lowest temperature at which appplication of a test flame causes the vapors above the surface of melted wax to ignite. The flash point gives indication of the ease with which a melted wax will burn. As might be expected the flash point temperature of a wax goes up as the wax melting point is increased. This is shown in the following tabular data:

Wax M.P.,°F.	Flash Temp., °F.
120	395
130	405
140	425
150	465

To a degree, flash point indicates that the lower melting paraffin waxes burn with greater ease than higher melting waxes. Flammability is discussed in greater detail under the subject of candle wicking, and in the chapter on storage and handling of petroleum wax.

7. *Specific Heat and Latent Heat of Fusion*

Specific heat is the quantity of heat, expressed in B.T.U., required to raise the temperature of one pound of substance one degree Fahrenheit at a given temperature. For wax in the liquid state, specific heat may be calculated from the following formula:
$$S = 0.476 + 0.0005t$$
where t is the temperature of the wax in °F., and S is the specific heat of the wax at that temperature, in B.T.U. / Pound / °F.

Latent heat of fusion is the quantity of heat in B.T.U. absorbed by one pound of a solid while changing to a liquid at its melting point. The latent heat of fusion of paraffin waxes is estimated to be approximately 97 B.T.U. / lb.

These values may be used in a practical way to calculate the amount of heat required to raise the temperature of a given quantity of wax, to melt it, or to calculate the amount of heat to be removed to solidify it.

Table No. 2

PHYSICAL PROPERTIES OF TYPICAL CANDLE WAXES

	Wax B[4]	Wax D[4]	Wax E[4]	Blend H[4]
Melting Point, D-87°F.	127	131	140	133
Oil Content, D-721, %	1.3	0.4	0.2	0.4
Penetration Hardness, D-1321				
at 77°F	15	10	7	13
100°	130	45	13	73
110°	238	103	23	122
Kin. Viscosity, D-445, cs[5]				
at 160°F.	5.2	5.8	6.8	———
180°	4.2	4.5	5.5	———
210°	3.2	3.5	4.1	———
Typical Use	Vigil lights and candles cast in glass jars	Molded Pillar Candles	Dipped and molded Tapers	Foliating Pillar Candles

[4] Identification used for waxes discussed in following chapters in discussing production of specific candles.
Values given are rounded-off averages for the type wax.
[5] See Appendix.

5
Candle Wicking

Having covered information on the science of candles, including technology of paraffin wax, the wick must now be understood for a complete background of knowledge on candles.

Just as paraffin wax has been specially developed for candle use, so also has a variety of special wicking been developed for use in each of the many types of candles that are made. Wicking originally used in candles was a crudely twisted, non-uniform, cotton yarn. Wicking that is available today is uniform in each of three types and many sizes. To achieve desired candle performance, wick type and size should be balanced against wax properties as well as candle type and diameter. These relationships will be discussed in this chapter.

Wicks are used as a metering device for the melted wax as the candle is burned. Within each type of wick, size is selected to control burning rate for best candle performance. The larger the wick, the higher the burning rate with a given candle wax.

There are three types of candle wicking available for use: metal-core wick with a woven cotton sleeve, flat-plaited cotton wick, and square-braided cotton wick. As will be described, each wick type is made to self-adjust its height above the melted wax surface as the candle is burned. Thus, the candle snuffer is no longer needed to trim the wick when a properly made modern candle is burned. The wick continuously "snuffs" itself, and thus adjusts flame height by being shortened in the hot part of the flame. In each of the three different wicks this action is built into the wick in a way that is characteristic of each type. The construction of the three is as follows:

57

Metal-Core Wick, with woven cotton sleeve.

In this wick, lead wire is used as a core. In burning a candle with this type, the tip of the lead wire melts in the hot outer part of the flame, beads of melted lead repeatedly drop off, and the cotton sleeve is consumed in the flame. This action effectively shortens the wick in a continuous fashion as the candle is burned.

Metal-core wicking is used principally in candles that are burned in glass containers. The metal core provides rigidity to the wick that allows it to remain vertical when surrounded by a depth of melted wax. A wick with a low-melting polyethylene filament as a core has recently been made available as a modification of the lead-core wick. Both lead-core and polyethylene-core wicking act the same when the candle is burned. Use and performance of metal-core wick is discussed in detail in Chapter 7, as related to production of votive lights and related candles made in glass jars.

Flat-Plaited Wick

Early in the 19th century it was discovered that if a cotton wick was braided instead of twisted, it would tend to curl into the hot area of the candle flame where the tip can burn off to be continuously shortened. This discovery popularized the plaited cotton wick for present-day use. However, wick curl tends to broaden the flame, which puts the flame slightly off center in the direction of the curl. This could be a disadvantage in burning tapers and dinner-type candles. The off-center flame may lead to dripping and guttering. However, in large diameter candles an off-center flame may aid the unburned collar of wax to form petals. This is further discussed, under production of foliating or angel wing candles, in Chapter 9.

Flat-plaited wick is made mechanically using three groups of yarn made up of 3 to 12 or more strands, with 7 to 12 plaits per inch. Generally the finer the yarn count the more strands there are and the greater the number of plaits per inch. It is to be noted that the plait is formed into a downward "V" on one side of the flat and reversed on the other side. In burning a candle with this wicking, it will curl outward on the side on which the strands "V" downward.

All cotton wicking is specially treated for candle use by steeping in a salt solution. This treatment is termed pickling in the trade. It retards wick burning, eliminates after-glow when the flame is extinguished, and retards burning rate of the wax, which tends to reduce soot formation. A typical salt solution used for pickling the wicking contains ammonium phosphate, ammonium sulfate, and sodium borate dissolved in water. Hanks of wicking are steeped in the salt solution for about 24 hours, drained, dried, and then wound onto bobbins for use. Guides to size selection and specific use of the plaited flat wicking are discussed in greater detail in the several chapters on candle manufacture.

Square-Braided Wicking

This wicking is almost square in cross section and as such has less tendency to hook or curl in the candle flame. The tip of the square wick burns off in the hot area at the top of the candle flame. In this way flame size is controlled. The square wick remains rather straight in the flame area of a burning candle. In this way a rather narrow flame is obtained in contrast to a more or less flared flame that is produced by a flat-plaited wick of the same size.

The square-braided wick is generally preferred for use in tapers and dinner candles to reduce tendency of the candle to drip or gutter when burned. It is especially useful in candles that are burned in spring-loaded cylindrical holders having a metal cap, for example, tavern candles. Square braided wicking is further discussed in the several chapters on candle manufacture.

Wick size and wax melting point as related to burning rate of the candle is presented along with discussion on each particular type candle in the respective chapters on candle production.

The major supplier of candle wicking in the United States is the Atkins and Pearce Company, Cincinnati, Ohio. A summary description of popular size Atkins and Pearce wicking is given in the Appendix. For less than large quantities of candle wicking there are many local candle wick distributors, some of which are listed in the Appendix.

6
Additives Used in Candle Wax

Substances that are mixed into paraffin wax for use in production of candles are known as additives. There are two principal reasons for additives in candle wax: to modify or improve candle appearance, and to modify or improve candle performance.

The presence of some additives are immediately apparent. For example, the many colorful candles seen in candle shops are produced by addition of wax-soluble dyes to the candle wax. The aromas evolved from candles are evidence that perfumes have been added. In addition to these obvious additives there are many that are not at all obvious by casual inspection of the finished candle. Included among these less apparent additives are those used to improve crystal structure, hardness, tensile and transverse breaking strength, ductility, or color stability of the wax. The quality of the base wax employed determines the need for these additives and the quantity that should be used.

In general, candle-wax additives are non-petroleum materials. When they are used, the resultant candle wax is known as a *composition*. When two or more dissimilar waxes are mixed together the resultant candle wax is known as a *blend*. For uniformity of composition it is essential that all additives be mutually soluble in the melted wax and be compatible with each other. Blended waxes must also be mutually soluble.

Notable among original candle-wax additives is stearic acid (see Chapter 3). Historically, it was probably the first used. It was employed to harden the soft paraffin waxes available to the early candle maker. Use of stearic acid was probably followed in time by blending dissimilar waxes—for example beeswax—with petroleum wax.

Additives generally have a specific use in candle wax, although there may be side effects that must also be considered. In this discussion all effects are to be looked at for each type of additive. For orientation each additive will first be briefly described. Following this, each will be discussed in greater detail, and then as groups for particular use, to provide a more useful reference.

Stearic Acid is used in amounts up to 30 percent in refined paraffin wax to harden the wax, improve rigidity of the candle—for reduction in tendency to sag at high temperatures—and to improve the opaqueness of the candle.

High-Melting Point Microcrystalline Wax is used as an additive in amounts up to 1 percent in close-cut paraffin wax and in semi-refined paraffin wax containing up to 1.5 percent oil. It is used to improve wax structure, to improve strength characteristics, and to eliminate snow spots (imperfections in appearance).

Polyethylene, low molecular weight, low density polyethylene—for example AC-6 polyethylene (Allied Chemical Co.)—is used in amounts up to about 2 percent to harden the wax, improve gloss of molded candles, and to improve structure. Its presence will reduce burning rate with a given-size wick and a given-melting-point wax.

Ethylene-Vinyl-Acetate Copolymer (EVA). An EVA having a 28 percent vinyl-acetate content and a high melt-index (low viscosity), is used principally for improving appearance and strength characteristics of dipped tapers. Use of EVA in wax employed to produce molded candles is not advised, as mold release may be made difficult. Elvax 210 (DuPont) is suggested for use in amounts up to about 1 percent in paraffin candle wax.

Fischer-Tropsch Wax—for example Paraflint RG (Moore and Munger)—is a synthetic, hard, high molecular weight wax-like material that is used in amounts up to 1 percent to improve crystal structure and strength characteristics of candles. It may be used in higher amounts, up to about 20 percent, in wax applied as a final coat for dipped candles to make them dripless.

Color and Oxidation Stabilizers are used in rather low concentrations to inhibit the wax against color and odor degradation. These additives are rather complex phenolic compounds. Some protect against wax color degradation by sunlight, others protect against degradation at elevated temperatures due to heat and oxygen by air.

Colorants are wax-soluble dyes employed to enhance the aesthetic appearance of candles. Pigments used in crayons are not soluble in paraffin wax and should not be used in candle wax. It is difficult to prepare a stable dispersion of pigments in candle wax, but more importantly pigments if used will clog the wick and impede candle burning.

Odorants are wax-soluble perfumes, generally used in conjunction with dyes, that give a colored candle an aroma associated with the color.

These additives are now to be discussed in greater detail, both individually and as groups for a given application.

Stearic Acid

This is an organic fatty acid with a condensed formula of $C_{17}H_{35}COOH$. Pure stearic acid has a 157° F. melting point and is soluble in all proportions in melted paraffin wax.

Petroleum wax, as used originally in making candles, was a soft and plastic substance. Fortunately stearic acid, isolated from animal fats, was found to harden the soft wax when the two were solidified together. The early enterprising candle maker capitalized on this discovery. In addition it was found that the presence of stearic acid in paraffin wax candles kept them from sagging when held in an upright position at elevated room temperature.

The stearic acid originally used was a crude mixture of saturated fatty acids. As knowledge and technology of fats increased, a pure, white stearic acid was made available for use. This grade—known in the trade as double pressed stearic acid—became the grade commonly used in candle wax. In addition to improving rigidity of candles, it was found to provide an attractive opaque white appearance to undyed solidified candle wax. Depending upon the quality and properties of the paraffin wax employed, as well as the candle appearance and performance desired, it became general practice to add 10 to 30 percent stearic acid to the candle wax. Commercial candles containing stearic acid were identified as stearine candles and have been marketed by this name.

Performance of stearic acid in a candle wax depends upon purity of the acid. As might be expected, the greater the purity, the higher its melting point. Thus, stearic acid is available in several melting point grades, commonly known as titre grades, ranging from about 130° up to about 150° F. The higher its purity and melting point, the better its performance.

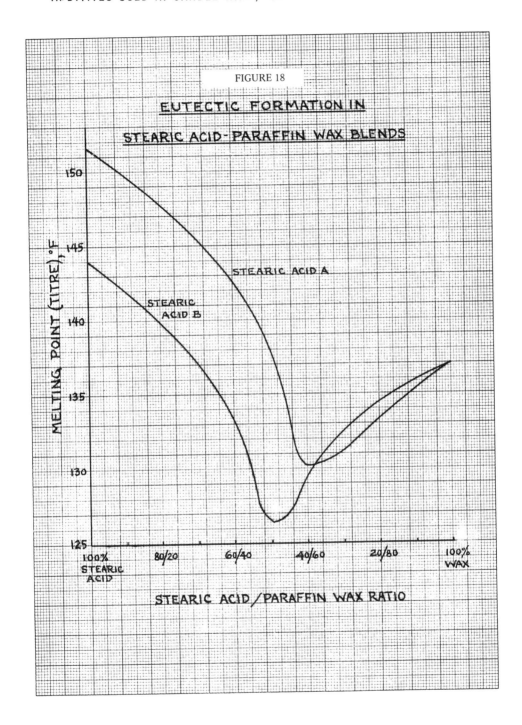

FIGURE 18

EUTECTIC FORMATION IN

STEARIC ACID-PARAFFIN WAX BLENDS

It is of interest to note that as a side effect, stearic acid lowers the melting point of the wax to which it is added. This lowering takes place through the formation of a eutectic, as shown in Figure 18. Wax-stearic acid eutectic formation is similar to formation of an alloy of two metals. It can be explained using Figure 18. Depending upon the original composition of a wax-stearic acid blend, when it cools from the liquid state to the solid state either stearic acid or wax initially separates until the eutectic composition is reached. At the eutectic point both wax and stearic acid jointly solidify as a single crystalline phase of constant ratio composition. For example, with 10 to 30 percent stearic acid in the 137° F. melting point paraffin wax, the wax will solidify out of the melt first until the eutectic composition is reached. With stearic acid A, having a 151.5° M.P. (titre), the eutectic point is reached at a composition comprising 40 percent stearic acid and 60 percent wax. With stearic acid B, having a 143.9° M.P., the eutectic composition comprises 48 percent stearic acid and 52 percent wax. With, for example, a composition comprising 30 percent 151.5° melting-point stearic acid and 70 percent 137° F. M.P. wax when cooled from the liquid to the solid state, free wax will solidify from the melt until the melt comprises 40 percent stearic acid—60 percent wax, which is the eutectic composition. At the eutectic point eutectic material solidifies as a single composition. With 10 to 30 percent stearic acid in the 137° F. M.P. wax, the higher melting-point stearic acid provides the advantage of allowing less free wax to separate before the eutectic is reached than when a lower melting point stearic acid is used. In addition, the eutectic composition has a higher melting point and contains less stearic acid when the higher-melting stearic acid is used.

The chart in Figure 18 also shows that the presence of stearic acid lowers the melting point of a paraffin wax. Nevertheless, the presence of stearic acid decreases the tendency for a candle to sag at elevated temperature. This surprising fact is shown in Table No. 3, using a 141.2° F. melting point wax.

Table No. 3

SAG OF TAPERS[1] AT 100°F. DURING 32 HOURS

Wax Composition	Melt. Point, D-87, °F.	Sag, 1/16th Inch
Base Paraffin Wax	141.2	34
Base Wax + 10% Stearic Acid A	139.5	20
Base Wax + 20% Stearic Acid A	138.1	11
Base Wax + 10% Stearic Acid B	139.7	21
Base Wax + 20% Stearic Acid B	138.0	11

[1] An accelerated test in which 12-inch-long tapers of similar diameter, clamped at the base and extended the same distance in a horizontal position, are allowed to sag in a 100°F. oven during 32 hours of time.

A disadvantage to the use of stearic acid in a white candle wax is that it may degrade color and color stability of the wax and cause the candle to prematurely yellow. This is shown in an accelerated test in which the wax is exposed to high intensity ultraviolet light, as shown in Table No. 4.

Table No. 4

5-HOUR ULTRAVIOLET LIGHT COLOR STABILITY

Wax Composition	A.S.T.M. Color[2]	
	Original Wax	5 Hr. Exposure
Base 141.2°F. M.P. Wax	+30	+18
Base Wax + 10% Stearic Acid A	+23	+11
Base Wax + 20% Stearic Acid A	+20	+10
Base Wax + 10% Stearic Acid B	+24	+11
Base Wax + 20% Stearic Acid B	+20	+10

[2] A +30 color is a pure white wax. The lower the number the more yellow there is in the color.

High Melting-Point Microcrystalline Wax

This is a petroleum wax that contains a high percentage of iso-paraffins and arbitrarily has a melting point above about 170° F. It is used as an additive in close-cut paraffin waxes and semi-refined paraffin waxes (with up to 1.5 percent oil content) to improve crystalline structure and eliminate snow spots. In addition to improving structure and appearance of a paraffin wax, microcrystalline wax also improves tensile and transverse breaking strength. Generally no more than 0.5–1.0 percent microcrystalline wax need be added to markedly correct a poor structured wax and produce a fine grained appearance without blemishes. This approach is effective in semi-refined waxes that are used to make candles molded in glass jars.

To improve strength characteristics of a refined paraffin wax may require as much as 5 percent addition of high-melting micro-crystalline wax. This may be practiced in producing self-supported tapers and molded dinner candles where high strength characteristics are required. However, when a candle wax contains 5 percent high-melting microcrystalline wax, a slightly larger than normal-sized wick may have to be used to compensate for a degree of wick plugging that may take place by the high melt wax.

Polyethylene

Polyethylene is a synthetic white opaque plastic produced from ethylene gas by controlled polymerization. The plastic is available in pellets for convenience. It has a chemical structure similar to paraffin wax but most often has a much higher carbon number and wider carbon number distribution. A low molecular weight grade (c. 2,000), having a rather low melting point (c. 210° F.) and a low density (c. 0.92), is most suitable for addition to candle wax. AC-6 polyethylene meets these requirements. It is readily dissolved in paraffin wax at a temperature of about 220° F. It will, however, tend to haze in paraffin wax at a temperature of about 160° F. Higher melting polyethylenes are more difficult to dissolve in paraffin wax and have a higher haze temperature. Both conditions may be troublesome.

AC-6 polyethylene in amounts up to about 2 percent in paraffin wax will harden a soft wax, improve gloss of molded candles, and improve strength characteristics of these candles. However, polyethylene has a much lower volatility than does paraffin wax, thus it will tend to accumulate in the wick when the candle containing the polyethylene is burned. This accumulation reduces the burning rate with a given-size wick. To compensate for this effect a slightly larger wick may be used to maintain a required burning rate. Relationship between wick size and burning rate of molded tavern candles, made with a 145° F. melting point paraffin wax containing 1 percent AC-6 polyethylene, is shown in Table No. 5.

Table No. 5

CANDLE BURNING RATE

Of Candles made with 145°F. M.P. Paraffin Wax +1% AC-6
Using Atkins and Pearce Square Braided Wicking
in Molded Tavern Candles

Wick Size[3]	Wax	Burning Rate Grams per Hour
6/0	Base Wax	4.4
6/0	Wax + 1% AC-6	4.3
5/0	Base Wax	5.7
5/0	Wax + 1% AC-6	5.5

[3] Note the 5/0 wick is slightly larger than the 6/0 wick.

Ethylene-Vinyl Acetate Copolymer (EVA)

EVA is a white somewhat translucent resin, made by polymerizing ethylene and vinyl acetate together. A resin synthesized of two or more component chemicals is known as a copolymer. The ratio of one component to the other in the copolymer, as well as the extent of polymerization, determines the properties and thus the suitability of the resin for use in candle wax. DuPont Elvax 210, an ethylene-vinyl-acetate copolymer with a 28 percent vinyl-acetate content and a low viscosity (high melt index), is an effective additive for candle wax.

Use of 0.5 to 1.0 percent of Elvax 210 in a 130° or 140°F. melting point paraffin wax produces candles with improved crystal structure, appearance, and strength characteristics over candles made with the straight base wax. Appearance and strength characteristics of candles made with a paraffin wax containing as little as 0.5 percent Elvax 210 compare favorably with similar candles made with the same base wax containing 10 to 20 percent stearic acid. In addition, use of Elvax in place of stearic acid has a cost advantage as well as allowing improved color stability. Color stability comparison is shown in Table No. 6.

Table No. 6

5-HOUR ULTRAVIOLET LIGHT COLOR STABILITY

Wax Composition	A.S.T.M. Color[4]	
	Original Wax	5 Hr. Exposure
Base 141.2°F. M.P. Wax	+30	+18
Base Wax + 0.5% Elvax 210	+30	+14
Base Wax + 10% Stearic Acid A	+23	+11
Base Wax + 20% Stearic Acid A	+20	+10

[4] A +30 color is a pure white wax. The lower the number the more yellow there is in the color.

The presence of Elvax 210 in candle wax does however reduce the burning rate of the candle wax. This can be adjusted by selection of a suitable size wick to obtain the burning rate and candle performance desired. This is shown in Table No. 7.

Table No. 7

CANDLE BURNING RATE

Of Candles made with 130°F. M.P. Paraffin Wax + 0.5% Elvax 210
Using Several Sizes of Atkins and Pearce Wicking
In 12"-long Dipped Tapers

Wax	6/0 TT Sq. Wick Burn Rate[5]	6/0 TT Sq. Wick Drip[6]	6/0 Sq. Wick Burn Rate	6/0 Sq. Wick Drip	15-Ply Plaited Wick Burn Rate	15-Ply Plaited Wick Drip
130°F. M.P. Wax	5.0	1.8	6.1	0.3	6.4	0.2
Base Wax + 0.5% Elvax 210	5.0	None	5.9	None	6.2	None

[5] Burn Rate in grams per hour.
[6] Drip value given in grams.
Note. 15-ply plaited wick is larger than the 6/0 square-braided wick and the 6/0 wick is larger than the 6/0 TT wick.

Use of Elvax 210 in wax employed to produce molded candles is not advised, as its presence tends to make the candles stick in the molds. Elvax 210 is most suitable for use in wax employed to produce dipped tapers. An amount of Elvax 210 up to 1 percent may be used in dipped candle wax with beneficial effects.

Fischer-Tropsch Wax

Fischer-Tropsch Wax is a paraffin wax synthesized from carbon monoxide and hydrogen at high pressure in the presence of a catalyst. Hard, high-melting fractions are isolated from the composite product and known in the trade as F.T. Waxes and Paraflint. They are useful in candle wax to raise melting point, improve structure and appearance, and increase hardness. A 1 to 2 percent addition of F.T. Wax is effective for this purpose.

Typical properties of selected Fischer-Tropsch waxes are:

	Congeal. Pt., °F.	Penetration Hardness (100 grams, 5 sec., 77°F.)
F.T.–200 Wax[7]	198° ± 4°	3 to 5
F.T.–300 Wax[7]	208° ± 3°	Below 1
Paraflint R.G.[8]	ca 204°	1 to 2

[7] Dura Commodities Corp.
[8] Moore and Munger Co.

Due to its high melting point and limited solubility in petroleum wax, the presence of Fischer-Tropsch wax in paraffin candle wax contributes a haze temperature of about 220° F. In this respect F.T. wax is subject to the same concentration limitations as is poly-ethylene in candle wax. The best use for F.T. wax is as a component in the final coat applied to a dipped candle or as a finishing coat to a molded candle. The hard high-melting finish coat gives the candle a glossy appearance and reduces the tendency of the candle to gutter or drip when burned. This coating may contain as much as 10 percent Paraflint, which amounts to less than 1 percent in the total candle. A low-melting, rather soft paraffin wax may thus be used for the major portion of the candle. A hard, high-melting coat on a soft, low-melting paraffin wax candle will retain melted wax, as in a cup, when the candle is burned. In this way, and by use of a wick of balanced size, a small pool of melted wax is retained at the base of the flame without dripping or guttering down the side of the candle. The hard outer coat is then gradually dissolved in the pool of melted wax as it is warmed by the flame.

Direct use of 1 to 2 percent Fischer-Tropsch wax in the entire candle wax requires wick size adjustment to allow for viscosity increase and slight wick plugging (see Chapter 5 on candle wicking).

Additives by Type of Use

In addition to the additives previously discussed, there are other types that are best discussed as a group by function for which they are used. These include color and oxidation stabilizers, a general discussion on crystal structure improvement by additives, mold release agents, colorants, and odorants. Discussion of these is as follows:

A. *Color and Oxidation Stabilizers* are generally aromatic compounds that preferentially absorb color degrading ultraviolet light, or hinder reaction with oxygen at elevated temperatures, to protect paraffin wax from light or heat color-degradation. Both light exposure of uninhibited white highly refined paraffin wax in the solid state, or heat exposure in the melted state in the presence of air, will contribute yellowing. Each of the two types of inhibitors are rather specific in performance.

1. *Ultraviolet light color stabilizers* include Tinuvin P (Geigy Chem. Corp.) and Cyasorb UV-531 (American Cyanamid Corp.). The chemical structure of these two additives is as follows:

Tinuvin P 2 (2'-hydroxy 5' methyl phenyl) benzotriazole.

Cyasorb UV-531   2-Hydroxy-4-n-octoxy benzophenone

Improvement in color stability by the presence of small quantities of either inhibitor in each of three typical candle waxes is shown in Table No. 8. These inhibitors are used in the wax in parts per million-parts of wax (abbreviated as ppm; 1 ppm is equal to 0.0001 percent).

Wax color is determined before and after five hours of standardized ultraviolet light exposure on a comparable basis. Color is measured by the A.S.T.M. method D-156, in which lower numbers indicate a darker color. In general, wax is stabilized against color darkening, due to light exposure, by the presence of 0.02 percent (200 ppm) of either inhibitor.

Table No. 8

5-HOUR ULTRAVIOLET LIGHT EXPOSURE[9]

Color Measured by A.S.T.M. D-156 Method

	Wax C[10]		Wax D[10]		Wax E[10]	
	Before	After	Before	After	Before	After
Base Case (no inhibitor)	+22	+7	+25	+13	+30	+10
25 ppm Tinuvin P	21	15	26	19	30	20
50 ppm Tinuvin P	21	14	26	21	30	21
100 ppm Tinuvin P	21	16	27	22	30	21
200 ppm Tinuvin P	21	19	27	22	30	22
25 ppm Cyasorb 531	21	14	30	18	30	16
50 ppm Cyasorb 531	21	13	30	20	30	19
100 ppm Cyasorb 531	22	12	28	22	30	19
200 ppm Cyasorb 531	22	14	28	21	30	21
25 ppm Tinuvin P / 25 ppm Cyasorb 531	—	—	30	20	—	—
50 ppm Tinuvin P / 50 ppm Cyasorb 531	—	—	27	22	—	—

[9] 5 Hours ± 3 min. exposure under 500-foot candles of light using a G.E. 275-watt sunlamp. Sample prepared in a glass Petri dish and removed to expose the smooth lower surface to the light in a darkened room. Saybolt color is measured on the original wax and again after exposure.

[10] See Table No. 2 for Physical Properties of these waxes.

2. *Elevated Temperature Oxidation Inhibitors* are generally the hindered phenol type, that reduce rate of oxidation of wax in the melted state. Included among these are Parabar 441 (Enjay) and Tenox BHA (Eastman Chemical Corp.). The chemical structure of these additives is as follows:

Parabar 441 Di-tert Butyl para Cresol (D.B.P.C.)
Synonym: Butylated Hydroxy Toluene (B.H.T.)

$$(CH_3)_3C \underset{CH_3}{\overset{OH}{\bigcirc}} - C(CH_3)_3$$

Tenox BHA Butylated hydroxy anisole, a mixture of two isomers (2 ter. butyl and 3 ter. butyl).

Examples of improved wax-oxidation stability provided by the presence of small quantities of either inhibitor in typical candle waxes is shown in Table No. 9.

Table No. 9

WAX HEAT STABILITY AT 270°F.[11]

	Hours to Rancidity			
	123°F. M.P. RFD. Wax	127°F. M.P. RFD. Wax	131°F. M.P. RFD. Wax	135°F. M.P. RFD. Wax
Base Case (no inhibitor)	2	2	2	2
15 ppm BHA	12	12	12	—
30 ppm BHA	13	13	13	—
50 ppm BHA	12	10	12	—
5 ppm DBPC	—	—	—	11

[11] 100 grams of wax in 500 cc Erlenmeyer flask in presence of 12 inches of bright No. 22 copper wire formed into a coil.

B. *Additives employed to Improve Crystal Structure* also provide a fine-grain appearance and improve strength characteristics in the finished candle.

Candles made by slow cooling of melted, highly normal, close-cut paraffin wax usually have a blemished non-uniform appearance in the solid state. Star-shaped imperfections known as "snow spots" form as air is squeezed out from the large plate-like crystals of the wax. Shock chilling the wax will form an unstable fine-grain structure with a superficial initial uniform appearance that gradually degrades with time, but snow spots are formed just the same. Shock chilling of large-size candles is never a good practice as a means for obtaining a fine-grained crystal structure when a close-cut normal paraffin wax is used. Structural strains and possibly cracks will form by shock chilling, especially in large candles. Surface wax solidifies into fine-grained crystals at first, but the solidified surface wax acts as an insulator so that internal cooling takes place at a slower rate. This allows large plate-like crystals to form in the internal structure of the candle. The large wax crystals in the interior of the candle gradually influence the fine-grained surface crystals to grow and conform, but in so doing internal strains and surface snow spots are gradually formed.

The best control for formation of fine grained, good-structured candles is by use of high-melting additives rather than by shock chilling. These additives include a variety of high-melting waxes, polymers, and resins. They function through their high melting point and very small crystal structure in the solid state. When present in melted wax these additives crystallize first as small needles when the melt is cooled and impress their form on the close-cut normal paraffins. A uniformly fine-grained, good-appearing candle with good strength characteristics is thereby produced.

Among large candles that are generally slow cooled in air and in which appearance may be critical, are seven-day votive lights casted in glass jars, and large diameter pillar candles casted in a variety of molding materials. To provide a fine-grained, good-appearing structure to these candles any one of the following additives may be effectively used.

1. A microcrystalline wax with a melting point of at least 170° F.
2. A low molecular weight polyethylene, for example AC–6.
3. A low viscosity, Ethylene-Vinyl Acetate copolymer, for example Elvax 210.
4. A high-melting, hard, Fischer-Tropsch wax, for example Paraflint RG.

In most cases use of as little as 1 percent of any one of these additives in a poor structured wax effectively produces a fine-grained structure in the finished candle. It is interesting to note that a "semi-microwax," containing 35 to 40 percent iso-paraffins and having a 150° F. melting point, may also be used for producing a fine-grained crystal structure. A concentration of about 10 percent is needed in the paraffin wax to be equally as effective as 1 percent of a 170° F. melting point microwax. This is discussed in production of votive lights and in production of large-diameter pillar candles.

Care should be taken to control the concentration of high-melting additives in candle wax to the minimum required for structure adjustment. It should be remembered that these additives have lower volatility than the major portion of candle wax. As such they tend to accumulate in the wick, char, and impede capillarity. This reduces burning rate and in an extreme may cause burning failure. However, the presence of high-melting-point additives in candle wax may be compensated for by using a slightly larger wick as described in Chapter 5 on Candle Wicking.

C. *Additives to Improve Mold Release of candles* comprise additives that are not completely soluble in solidified candle wax. As such they exude a thin film of lubricant to the wax surface upon solidification in the candle mold. This film then aids release of the candle from the mold.

Mold release agents that may be used in the wax composition include hydrogenated rape seed oil (Archer, Daniels, Midland Co.) and fatty amides, for example Amide U (Humko Co., Oleamide). About 2 percent of these additives may be used to improve release of a candle wax that normally tends to stick in molds.

Wiping molds with a white mineral oil, or applying a spray coating of a silicone, may also be useful in improving mold release.

D. *Colorants* for candle wax should be wax-soluble dyes and should not be insoluble pigments or lakes, as are used in crayons. If the colorant is not soluble in the wax it will accumulate in the wick when the candle is burned. As with non-volatile additives, accumulation of pigment in the wick will retard capillary action and starve or possibly extinguish the flame. In addition, use of insoluble pigments presents a problem in obtaining a uniform colorant dispersion in the wax.

To insure complete solubility of dye, a concentrate may first be made in melted wax, then fine-cloth filtered at elevated temperature. The concentrate is then used in the quantity necessary to obtain the coloration required in the finished candle. It is to be noted that dye concentration required must be judged in the completely solidified finished candle if an exact color intensity or tint is to be obtained. Use of two or more dye concentrates is a convenient method for blending colors to obtain pale shaded tints in the finished candle.

E. *Odorants* for candle wax are generally employed to provide an aroma that will match a color given to the wax. Some odorants, as for example citronellal, are used to provide a degree of insect repellency with the vapors that are produced when the candle is burned. The odorant or perfume should be completely soluble in the wax to obtain best odor retention and to avoid degradation of crystal structure evidenced by a dull appearance or possibly snow spot formation. In extreme cases of incompatibility the odorant may exude to the surface and evaporate with eventual loss of odor.

To obtain a subtle aroma level a minimum concentration of odorant should always be employed. Generally, a 0.1 to 0.2 percent concentration of odorant in wax is ample to produce the desired aroma. The wax in which the odorant is employed may influence performance. Generally a wax with greater than 1 percent oil content will retain the odorant very well, but the candle appearance will be poor unless an additive to improve structure is used. For this purpose a concentration of about 1 percent of a 170° F. melting point microwax may be used. Otherwise a wax with an isoparaffin content of about 10 percent is suggested for improved odorant performance in a paraffin wax. Fatty amides, for example oleamide (Humko Amide U) may also be used to improve compatibility and retention of an odorant. However, it is best practice to determine exact formulation experimentally to obtain the result desired.

Suppliers of candle wax odorants and perfumes are listed in the Appendix.

Wax Blends to provide required Plasticity

Candles produced by hydraulic extrusion, screw extrusion, or compression molding of powdered wax are required to possess a built-in amount of plasticity. Plasticity may be measured by penetration hardness (A.S.T.M. D–1321) at a given temperature, along with change in hardness as the temperature is changed. Both are important in defining required plasticity.

Performance properties of the finished candle, principally burning quality, are controlled for the most part by melting point of the wax. Plasticity of the wax for the given melting point is controlled by adjusting its isoparaffin content. Two waxes having essentially the same melting point, but having a widely different isoparaffin content, may be blended to achieve an intermediate plasticity as shown in Table No. 10.

Table No. 10

	Wax I	Wax II	50:50 Blend Wax I & Wax II
Melting Point, D-87, °F.	122.4	123.6	122.2
Oil Content, D-721, %	1.3	1.9	1.6
H.C. Anal. by Mol. Sieve			
% Normal Paraffins	94	63	78
% Isoparaffins	6	37	22
Pen. Hardness, D-1321, 0.1 mm			
at 77°F.	13	68	39
100°	166	250	245
110°	175	——	326

A wax having a required melting point with a penetration hardness value at a given temperature may be duplicated if the melting point and isoparaffin content are known. For an example see Table No. 11.

Table No. 11
Duplication of a Wax by Blending

	Required Wax	Possible Component Waxes		Blend 50:50	
		Wax III	Wax IV	Wax III	Wax IV
Melting Point, D-87, °F	150	151	150	150	
H.C. Anal. by Mol. Sieve[12]					
% Normal Paraffins	64	88	40	64	
% Isoparaffins	36	12	60	36	
Pen. Hardness, D-1321, 0.1 mm					
at 100°F.	30	13	70	32	

[12] Molecular Sieve Analysis

Wax composition to approximate the required 30 penetration value at 100° F. is calculated from component isoparaffin contents as follows:

Wanted: 36 percent isoparaffin content, by blending two waxes, one with 12 percent isoparaffin content and the other having 60 percent isoparaffins. Take the difference in isoparaffins between Wax III and that required, as the amount of Wax IV. Conversely the difference in isoparaffins between Wax IV and the amount required, is the amount of Wax III to be used.

Thus, 60 percent — 36 percent = 24 parts Wax III

36 percent — 12 percent = 24 parts Wax IV

This then is a 50:50 blend on a 100 percent basis.

Production of a wax blend to have a given melting point and penetration values is best achieved as a bicomponent composition of waxes having essentially the same melting point but differing only in isoparaffin content. Blending of two or more dissimilar melting point waxes, to obtain required penetration values, most often leads to a compromise. Two examples are given, one in Table No. 12, the other in Table No. 13.

Table No. 12
Bicomponent Blend

	Required Wax	Possible Component Waxes		Blend 10% Wax V, 90% Wax VI
		Wax V	Wax VI	
Melting Point, D–87, °F.	130–132	145	130	130.6
Pen. Hardness, D–1321, 0.1 mm				
at 77°F.	9	30	6	8
100°	73	95	84	52
100°	123	210	144	115

These data indicate that penetration values do not blend arithmetically.

Table No. 13
Difficulty in Wax Blending

	Required Wax	Component Waxes			Tri-Component Blend 5% Wax VII 55% Wax VIII 40% Wax IX
		Wax VII	Wax VIII	Wax IX	
M.P., D-87, °F.	132	97	123	150	133
Pen. / 77°F.	13	90	13	16	22
100°F.	97	(melted)	95	35	116
110°F.	141	(melted)	120	45	213
Iso-Par., %	19	2	5	36	18

It should be noted that the low-melting component dominates softening of the blend at temperatures above its melting point.

Blending of widely dissimilar waxes is not recommended as a means for duplicating penetration values at a series of temperatures. In this instance blending by melting point and isoparaffin content to obtain required penetration values is not possible.

7
Jar-Lites

The Jar-Lite is the simplest variety of candle that may be made. It is particularly well suited for production by the home hobbyist. First select an attractive or purposeful glass container in which to make the candle. To allow the wick to be equidistant from any point on the side wall, in a given horizontal plane, the container should be circular in cross section. Plain or fancy glass tumblers, brandy snifters, or glass jars are among the containers that may be used. Seven-day votive lights made in glass jars for use in religious worship are included among this type of candle.

Metal core wicking having a degree of rigidity should be used in Jar-Lites. In setting up the wick it is crimped into a thin metal plate at the bottom end, then centered in the glass container. A wire clip arranged at the top of the container is used to hold the wick in a centered position. Melted wax is then poured into the glass or jar and allowed to solidify. If the wax in solidifying develops a cavity around the wick, it is to be filled with additional wax to provide an initially level surface for the candle. With the wax thoroughly solidified and cooled to room temperature, the wire clip is removed from the top of the jar, whereupon a finished candle is ready for use. The sketches in Figure 19 illustrate the sequence of steps used in making this type of candle.

Many commercial candles may be classified as Jar-Lites. Among them, those in greatest production are seven-day votive lights, tumbler and brandy snifter lights, and candles made in candy and pill jars. Machine-molded candles, made to be burned in glass containers, are another type of candle to be discussed in Chapter 9.

Among Jar-Lites the seven-day votive light is probably in greatest commercial production. Therefore, the details in producing this

STEP ONE - PLACE END OF
SUITABLE LENGTH OF METAL CORE
WICK THROUGH STAR CUT IN WICK
TIN AND BEND TIPS OF STAR DOWN
TO HOLD WICK IN PLACE. } SEE FIGURE 5

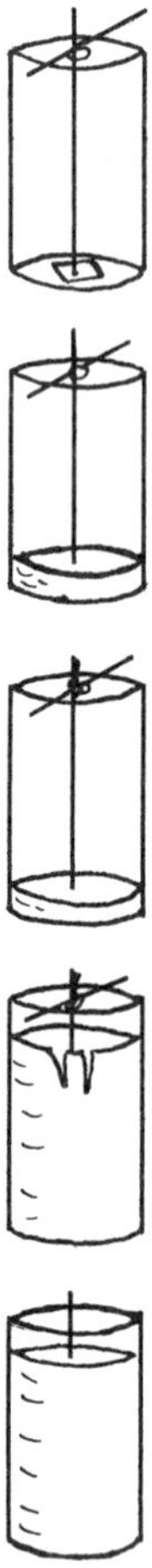

STEP TWO- PLACE WICK AND WICK
TIN IN JAR WITH WICK CENTERED
BY LOOP IN WIRE ROD PLACED
ACROSS TOP OF JAR.

STEP THREE - POUR ¼" TO ½"
DEPTH OF WAX INTO JAR AND
ALLOW TO SOLIDIFY. THIS POUR
IS KNOWN AS THE TACK POUR.

STEP FOUR - PULL WICK UP TO
STRAIGHTEN AND LOOP IT AROUND
THE ROD TO HOLD IT CENTERED
IN THE JAR.

STEP FIVE - MAKE MAJOR POUR
OF WAX TO FILL JAR TO WITHIN
¼" TO ½" OF TOP. ALLOW WAX
TO SOLIDIFY.

STEP SIX - PROBE FOR CAVITIES BELOW
SURFACE OF THE WAX IN THE WICK
AREA. FILL CAVITIES WITH WAX
AND PROVIDE A LEVEL SURFACE TO
THE CANDLE.

STEP SEVEN - REMOVE WIRE ROD
AND TRIM WICK TO A ½" TO ¾"
LENGTH ABOVE TOP OF CANDLE.

FIGURE 19

Three stages of pouring a jar candle (Courtesy Atlantic Richfield Co., Phila., Pa.)

candle may be used to point out and illustrate procedures and problems common to all Jar-Lites.

In the seven-day votive light, as with all Jar-Lites, the size and shape of the jar is first to be considered. As will be described, the diameter and shape of the jar have a definite influence upon the performance of the candle. The wax that is to be used must be defined by physical properties in order to meet the requirements of the candle manufacturer and the candle user. Then last, but not least, the wick size must be chosen to provide performance balance with the wax. In the seven-day votive light, for example, burning time and burning quality must be designed into the candle. How this is done is now to be considered.

Seven-day Votive Lights

To begin with there are many types of votive-light jars, as shown in Figure 20. Jar diameter is as important as shape. Wide-mouth construction or narrow-mouth construction, constricted side

Types of wide-mouth candle jar (Courtesy Atlantic Richfield Co., Phila., Pa.)

wall or straight side wall—all have an influence upon the burning quality of the candle. For example, in burning a candle made in a narrow-mouth jar, heat that accumulates within the jar melts surface wax. When a wide-mouth jar is used less heat is reflected to melt the wax. However, as the candle in the narrow mouth jar burns down toward the bottom there may be less oxygen from the air able to get to the flame to support good combustion. When this happens soot may be produced with reduction in flame temperature. Heat accumulated within the jar also depends upon burning rate of the candle, which is controlled by wick size and wax melting point.

Before further discussion on details of the interrelated factors —wick, wax and jar type—let us first consider the mechanics in burning this type of candle. When a seven-day votive light is burned, accumulated heat should produce a layer of melted wax at the base of the flame. This melted wax should extend across the entire wax surface to the jar wall. A hole should not be burned down into the wax, as this leaves unburned wax on the jar wall. This unburned wax on the jar wall not only reduces potential burning time, it may finally melt down to cover the wick and extinguish the flame. Either is faulty performance. With a layer of melted wax preferred in burning a Jar-Lite, the wick must be rigid enough to remain vertical and support the flame above the wax surface. If the wick were not rigid it would fall over into the melted wax and the flame would be extinguished. This is avoided by using a metal core wick that provides sufficient rigidity to hold the wick upright.

Size of the metal core wick and melting point of the wax influence flame size, or burning rate, both of which determine the rate of heat production to melt the wax. The larger the wick, or the lower the melting point of the wax, the larger the flame and the higher the rate of heat production. But there is a limit. An excessively large flame will soot due to lack of sufficient oxygen

Types of narrow-mouth candle jar (Courtesy Atlantic Richfield Co., Phila., Pa.)

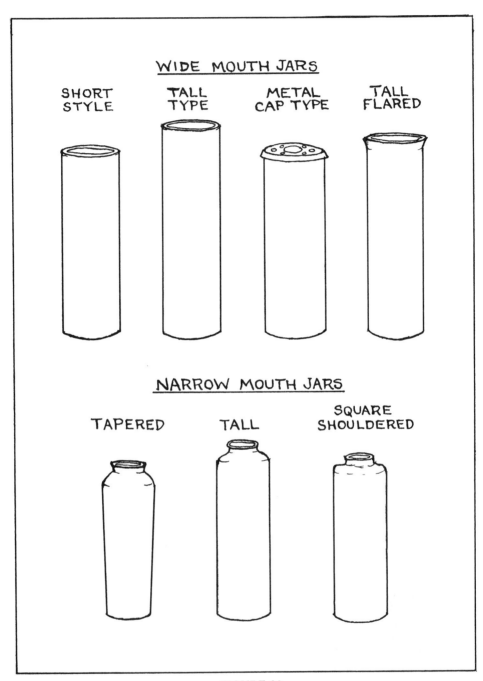

FIGURE 20

from the air in the jar to provide complete combustion. The up-draft of hot gases from combustion hinders diffusion of air into the jar and thereby starves the flame of oxygen. If the wick is too small or the melting point of the wax is too high, the flame is small and heat output is reduced to a point wherein a hole will be burned down into the wax by the candle flame. While this situation avoids soot formation, considerable wax remains unburned on the jar wall. Both soot and unburned wax hung up on the jar wall are to be avoided. Influence of wick size upon candle burning performance is shown graphically in Figure 21. Influence of wax melting point upon burning rate is shown in Figure 22.

Wick arrangement and diameter of jar are also important in avoiding hang-up of wax on the jar wall. An off-center wick, even if of correct size for the wax being used, will tend to favor melting wax from the wall to which it is nearest and allow wax to remain on the opposite wall. This shows the importance of centering the wick in the jar when the candle is made. In addition, the larger the diameter of the jar the greater is the tendency for unburned wax to be left hanging on the jar wall. Jar diameter is thus to be included among the inter-related factors that influence performance of seven-day votive lights.

Specific details must be paid attention to for production of satisfactory seven-day votive lights. The trade requires that a candle will burn at least six days—preferably seven days—without hang-up of unburned wax and without production of soot.

Insofar as the wax influence is concerned, the melting point should be low enough to allow total consumption of the wax in burning the Jar-Lite. Seven-day votive lights are generally made with 127° F. melting point paraffin wax containing 1.0 to 1.5 percent oil. Use of a 34–40 metal core wick (42 to 45 mil. diam.) with this wax provides an excellent votive light in a wide variety of standard jars. Both soot formation and hang-up are at a minimum. With 600 grams (1.3 pounds) of wax in the jar it will burn for approximately six and one-half days.

Reference is made to a study of votive lights made in standard wide-mouth jars having a straight side wall and being 3″ inside diameter, 8″ high. Candles were made with three melting point grades of wax and four sizes of metal core wick. Physical properties of the three waxes are given in Table No. 14, and candle burning

INFLUENCE OF WICK SIZE
UPON
CANDLE PERFORMANCE

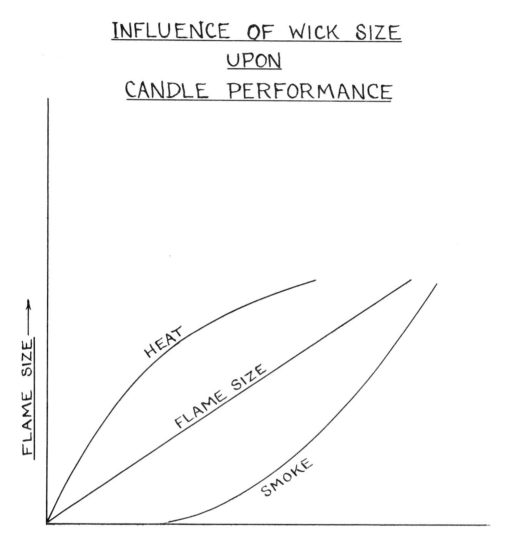

WICK SIZE ⟶

FIGURE 21

evaluations are summarized in Table No. 15. Burning rate is presented graphically in Figure 23, and soot formation is shown in Figure 24.

It has been shown that a votive light made in a 3″ inside

CANDLE BURNING RATE

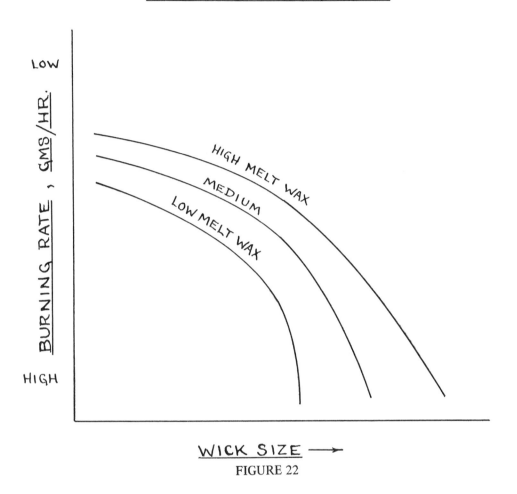

WICK SIZE ⟶

FIGURE 22

diameter jar with a 127° F. melting point wax and a 34–40 wick is a most satisfactory combination to avoid soot and hang-up. However, if the jar diameter is greater than 3 inches, with all other factors being the same, hang-up will occur, as shown in the following data.

Table No. 14

PHYSICAL PROPERTIES OF JAR-LITE WAXES

		Wax A	Wax B	Wax C
Wax M.P., D-87, °F.		124	127	135
Oil Content, D-721, %		1.3	1.3	1.2
Pen. Hardness, D-1321				
at 77°F.	=	12	15	16
100°F.	=	154	130	68
110°F.	=	Too Soft	238	162

Table No. 15

BURNING EVALUATION—"7-DAY" VOTIVE LIGHTS[1]
Wax vs. Metal-Core Wick Size

Wax M.P. °F.	Wick Size[2]	Burn. Rate gms./Hr.	Soot[3] Rating	Final Rating — Hang-up Rating, gms.
124	32–24	2.0	1	0
	34–40	4.5	2.5	0
	36–24–24	5.6	4.5	0
	44–32–18	7.6	5.0	0
127	32–24	1.9	0	2 (light)
	34–40	2.7	1	1 (very light)
	36–24–24	4.3	3	0
	44–32–18	6.9	4.5	0
135	32–24	1.9	0	63 (very heavy)
	34–40	2.2	0	30 (heavy)
	36–24–24	3.4	2	1 (very light)
	44–32–18	6.7	4.5	0

[1] Approximately 600 grams wax in standard wide mouth jar; (3″ inside diam. x 8″ high) Air Temperature 73°F.
[2] Wick description is given in the Appendix, part C.
[3] Numerical Qualitative Soot Rating:
   0=None
   1=Very Light
   2=Light
   3=Moderate
   4=Heavy
   5=Very Heavy

Jar Inside Diam., Inches	% Hang-up of Wax Burned[4]
2.7″ (68 mm)	none
3.0″ (76 mm)	nil
3.4″ (86 mm)	2 to 5%

[4] 127°F. M.P. wax, 34–40 metal core wick, wide-mouth jar with straight vertical sides. Air temperature 73°F.

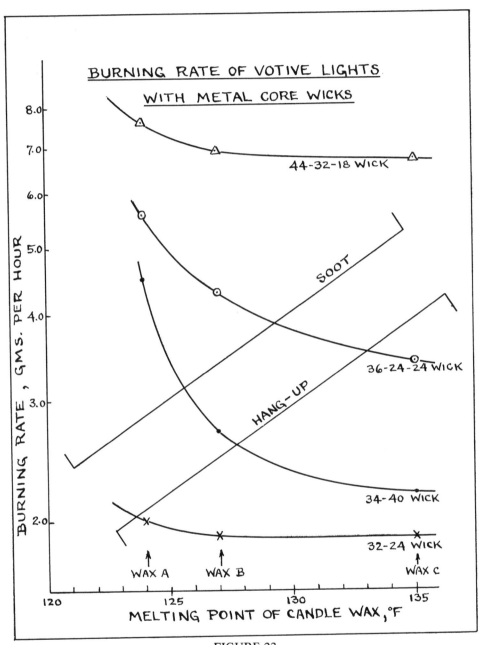

BURNING RATE OF VOTIVE LIGHTS
WITH METAL CORE WICKS

44-32-18 WICK

SOOT

36-24-24 WICK

HANG-UP

34-40 WICK

32-24 WICK

WAX A   WAX B   WAX C

BURNING RATE, GMS. PER HOUR

MELTING POINT OF CANDLE WAX, °F

FIGURE 23

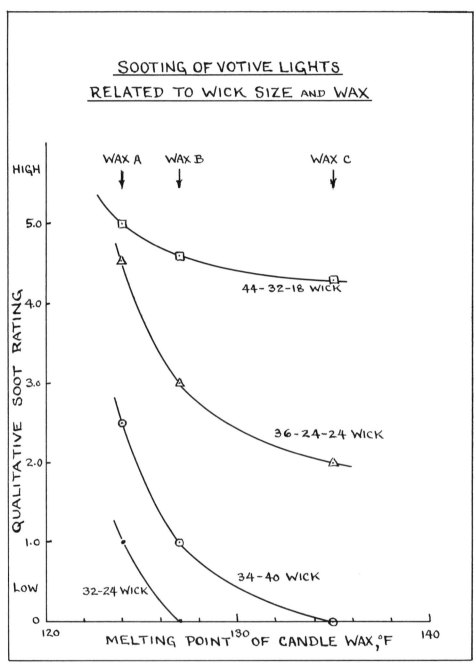

FIGURE 24

Hang-up may also occur if a 127° F. melting point wax is made by blending, for example:

Wax Type	% Hang-up of Wax Burned[5]
127° F. M.P. Wax	nil
Blend of 124°F. and 135°F. M.P. wax to a 127° Melting Point	5 to 6%

[5] 34–40 metal core wick, 3″ diameter wide-mouth jar with straight vertical sides. Air temperature 73°F.

Hang-up may, however, be reduced by employing a narrow-mouth jar in place of a wide-mouth jar when the blended 127° F. melting point wax is used. This is shown as follows:

Jar Type	% Hang-up of Wax Burned[6]
Wide mouth, 3″ ID	5 to 6%
Narrow mouth, 3″ ID	2 to 3%

[6] Blended 127°F. M.P. wax, 34–40 metal core wick. Air temperature 73°F.

In addition to the controllable factors pointed out, the temperature of the atmosphere in which the votive candle is burned may influence hang-up. For example, if the candle is burned in an unheated room during cold weather, hang-up most probably will result. In this instance hang-up in a wide-mouth jar caused by a cold atmosphere may be reduced by use of a perforated metal cap on the jar, as illustrated in Figure 25. The metal cap converts the wide-mouth jar to a narrow-mouth jar, wherein the cap reflects heat from the flame to melt surface wax and to melt down wax that would tend to hang-up on the jar wall.

To summarize, best burning performance is obtained with a seven-day votive light made as follows:

1. Use a wax having a 125 to 127° F. melting point.
2. Use a 34–40 metal core wick, well centered in the jar.
3. Use a narrow-mouth jar having an inside diameter no greater than 3 inches. To assure a burning time of no less than 168 hours (6 days) the jar should have a capacity for 600 grams (1.3 pounds) of wax.

Specific details in making a seven-day votive light are now to be considered. This candle may be made by a multiple wax pour method or by use of a premolded core containing the wick and one wax pour.

EXCESSIVE HANG-UP

Hang-up of unburned wax in candle jar (Courtesy Atlantic Richfield Co., Phila., Pa.)

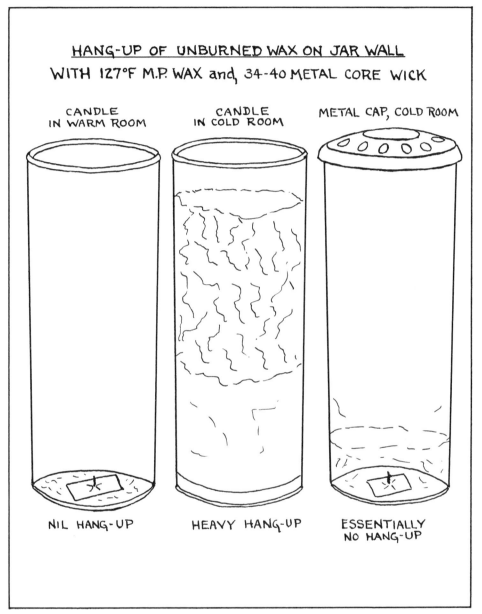

HANG-UP OF UNBURNED WAX ON JAR WALL
WITH 127°F M.P. WAX and 34-40 METAL CORE WICK

CANDLE
IN WARM ROOM

CANDLE
IN COLD ROOM

METAL CAP, COLD ROOM

NIL HANG-UP

HEAVY HANG-UP

ESSENTIALLY
NO HANG-UP

FIGURE 25

DETAILED MULTIPOUR METHOD FOR PRODUCING SEVEN-DAY VOTIVE LIGHTS

The first step is to prepare a sufficient quantity of prewaxed metal-core wicking by passing it back and forth in a bath of melted wax that is to be employed in the candle. An adequate length of prewaxed wicking is then arranged in the candle jar. The wick must be long enough to extend at least one-half inch above the anticipated top surface of the wax and allow crimping the other end into a metal base plate as previously shown in Figure 19. The base plate must be flat against the bottom of the jar, with the wick insert extending toward the side. In addition, the wick and wick-plate must be centered in the bottom. Melted wax is then poured into the jar to a depth of about one-half inch and allowed to solidify and cool. This layer of wax is known as the *tack-pour* in the trade. It is made to tack the wick into the bottom of the jar.

The wick is then pulled up straight, recentered, and held in position by means of a wire clip supported on the top of the jar. A major pour of melted wax is then made to fill the jar with sufficient wax to provide the burning time required.

All waxes contract during solidification while cooling to room temperature. Contraction of major pour wax, which takes place while adhering to the jar wall, causes a conical surface cavity to form around the wick. In some cases a subsurface hidden cavity may also form. Surface solidification takes place first, then subsurface cavities form during the final stages of cooling. To avoid initial burning problems, both types of cavities are to be filled with wax. If they are not, the candle flame will rapidly burn down into them only to be drowned by melting of surrounding wax. A level candle surface without a hidden cavity must be provided to avoid this candle burning fault.

After the major wax pour has solidified and cooled to room temperature, the presence of hidden cavities is explored. This is done by use of a pointed steel rod of about 1/8" diameter stock. Most hidden cavities occur in the wick area. It is therefore best to probe this area in several spots to uncover and open them so that they may be filled with wax. To finish the candle, the conical cavity and the hidden cavities are then filled with melted wax. In the trade this last pour is known as the *cap pour*.

Conical and hidden cavity formation may be minimized by controlling conditions that influence contraction, including pouring temperature, cooling rate, and melting point. Contraction is minimized by pouring the wax at as low a temperature as good conformation to the jar wall will allow. But, wax pouring temperature should not be so low as to cause the wax to solidify in ripples as it contacts the jar wall. With reduced contraction there is reduced cavity formation. A wax pouring temperature of 140° F. is suggested for a 125 to 127° F. melting point paraffin wax. Relationship between wax pouring temperature and the amount of contraction that takes place is shown in the following data:

Weight Percent Contraction[7] with 127°F. M.P. Wax
(Jars at 73°F. and candles cooled in 73°F. air)

Wax Pouring Temp. °F.	% Surface Cavity	% Hidden Cavity	% Total Cavity
140°	5.2	1.3	6.5
160°	6.5	2.0	8.5

[7] % Contraction based on total wax in jar. Candle made with three pours. Weight of third pour used to fill cavities and level the candle surface was determined.

Cooling rate most often is not controlled. For most part it depends upon pouring temperature and ambient room temperature. The greater the difference between the two temperatures, the higher the cooling rate in terms of heat loss per unit of time. However, some candle manufacturers slow down the wax cooling rate by having the candle jars contained in corrugated shipping boxes and pouring the wax at as low a temperature as is practicable. By this procedure there is less adherence of wax to the jar wall, with less conical contraction, and essentially no hidden cavities. This is shown with 127° F. melting point wax as follows:

Weight Percent Contraction with 127°F. M.P. Wax
(Wax Pouring Temperature 140°F.)

Cooling Method	% Surface Cavity	% Hidden Cavity
Cooled in 73°F. air	5.2	1.3
Cooled in shipping box	2.5	None

It is thus seen that slow cooling of 127° F. M.P. candle wax in making seven-day votive lights reduces conical surface cavity formation and eliminates hidden cavity formation. But, and there always seems to be a reservation, in slow cooling of a narrow cut wax there is a tendency for the wax to mottle and form snow spots as shown. Fortunately, as indicated in the discussion on additives, if snow spots occur they may be eliminated. Microwax, if added for crystal structure adjustment, should be held to a minimum to avoid an excessive surface cavity and critical reduction in burning rate. Influence of microwax concentration upon contraction of a 127° F. melting point wax is shown as follows:

Jars of mottled candle wax (Courtesy Atlantic Richfield Co., Phila., Pa.)

Weight Percent Contraction with 127°F. M.P. Wax
(127°F. M.P. Wax poured at 145°F., candles cooled in corrugated box)

% Microwax	% Surface Cavity	% Hidden Cavity
0	4.0	None
0.4%	4.7	None
0.9%	5.3	None

In summarizing the multipour method for making Jar-Lites, including seven-day votive lights, the following details should be observed:

1. A prewaxed metal-core wick should be used. Prewaxed for instant support of the candle flame, and metal core to provide rigidity to the wick when in a pool of melted candle wax.

2. The wick should be centered in the candle to provide uniform heat distribution for even melt down of wax from the jar wall.

3. Wick size should be balanced against melting point of the wax, and diameter of jar used. In a jar of up to 3 inches in diameter, a 125° F. to 127° F. melting point wax with 34–40 metal-core wick should be used.

4. Wax pouring temperature should be as low as is practicable, and wax cooling rate should be controlled to be as slow as possible to minimize cavity formation in the wick area.

5. Mottled and snow spot appearance that may develop in slow cooled wax may be eliminated by adding a small amount of a high-melting-point microwax.

USE OF A PREMOLDED CORE WITH WICK IN MAKING SEVEN-DAY VOTIVE LIGHTS

By centering a premolded candle core with wick in a candle jar, a finished seven-day votive light may be made with one pour of melted wax as shown in Figure 26. In this method cavity formation in the wick area is avoided. With care in placing the core within the jar and in making the wax pour, a candle with a level top surface and a centered wick is produced. Production of the premolded core is discussed in Chapter 9.

This procedure is well suited for use by commercial candle manufacturers. By this procedure production may be entirely automated. The cost of molding, wicking, filling, and packaging equipment may be paid for by increased production rate of quality candles. Production flow is shown in Figure 27.

As indicated in the flow sheet the operation is conducted stepwise. Candle cores are produced in automated molding equipment with prewaxed metal-core wick fed to the molding machine. A wicked core is then automatically placed and centered into each jar contained in a partitioned corrugated shipping carton. In the next operation a metered quantity of melted wax is run into each jar to fill the space between the core and the jar wall. The carton of candles is then conveyed to a cooling area, whereupon the procedure is repeated with the next carton of jars. As with candles made by the multipour method, the indicated balance between wick size, candle jar diameter, and wax melting point should be maintained.

CANDLES OTHER THAN VOTIVE LIGHTS THAT ARE BURNED IN GLASS JARS

Included among candles that are burned in glass jars are a

USE OF CANDLE CORE
IN MAKING VOTIVE LIGHT

CANDLE CORE
CENTERED IN JAR

FINISHED CANDLE
WITH LEVEL SURFACE

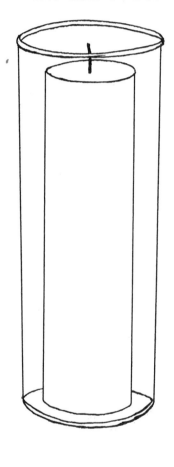

FIGURE 26

Varieties of paraffin wax candles. (*Courtesy Atlantic Richfield Co.*)

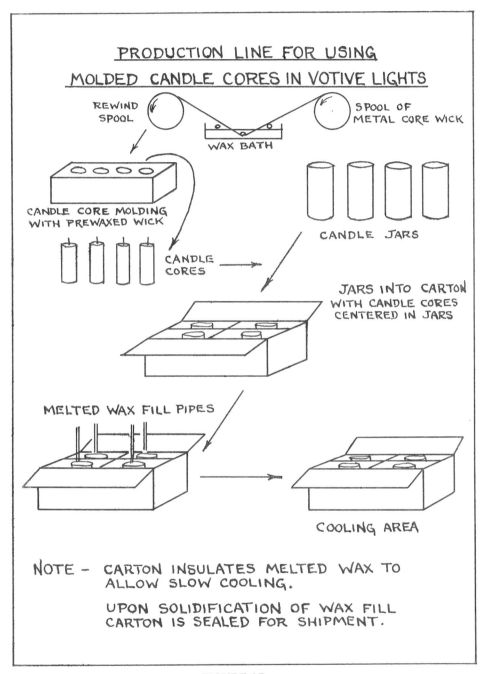

FIGURE 27

variety of premolded candles and candles that are made of wax particles packed around a metal-core wick.

The premolded candles include machine-molded vigil lights, warming candles, and varieties of perfumed candles. The candle hobbyist may use the jar in which the candle is to be burned to mold the candle and to make a supply of precise size and taper candle for use. For this purpose a jar with an outward taper is employed. The prepared and solidified candle is tapped out of the jar to supply the future use. Reference is made to Chapter 9 for discussion on machine-molded candles.

A 125° F. to 127° F. melting point paraffin wax and a 34–40 prewaxed metal-core wick are a satisfactory combination for use in making these candles. For special effects, dyes and perfumes may be used in the wax (refer to Chapter 6 on candle wax additives) .

In making candles with wax particles, wax chips, flakes, or beads are packed around a prewaxed metal-core wick centered in a glass jar, whereupon the candle is ready to be burned. Jar-Lites of wax particles may be made for sale as a kit. The kit would include a glass jar, a length of prewaxed metal core wick, a wick plate, and a package of wax particles. To guard against the tendency for the particles to stick together or "block" in the package, a rather high melting, normal paraffin wax should be used. To further insure against blocking, a quantity of AC–6 polyethylene, up to a concentration of 1 percent, may be employed in the wax. This type of wax has the added advantage of being more easily flaked or chipped in a mechanical chopper than a low-melting, highly isoparaffinic wax. Thus a wax with a melting point no lower than 130° F. and with no less than 90 percent normal paraffins is suggested. Either wax D or E described in Chapter 8 is suggested for chipping or flaking.

In all instances a prewaxed metal-core wick should be employed in candles burned in glass jars.

8
Dipped Tapers

Early approaches to mechanizing candle production were in dipping processes. A number of wicks were hung from a stick and repetitively dipped into melted wax to build up a candle around each wick. Wax picked up during each dip was allowed to solidify and harden before the next dip was made. Immediately after each dip the added layer of wax drained toward the bottom of the candle as it cooled to produce a gradual increase in diameter. The resultant candle was tapered, thus the name taper was given to dipped candles.

Most often early tapers were non-uniform in appearance and performance. Non-uniformity of the wick carried through the candle to give an exaggerated surface roughness. Waxes employed were variable in quality. Wax and air temperature were completely or essentially uncontrolled. Accordingly, the early candle makers of necessity employed practical craftsmanship to produce their wares. Modern present-day commercial candle manufacturers employ many controls to achieve high rate production of quality dipped candles. These controls are to be discussed.

The home hobbyist would also follow these basic controls if there is to be genuine pleasure in making dipped candles in a home work shop. A metal can, having a depth greater than the length of the candle to be made, is used to contain melted wax. A black iron can is best for this use; copper should not be used as it stimulates oxidation of the wax, which darkens it and gives it a burnt odor. A thermostatically controlled electrical hotplate is preferred as a source of heat to melt the wax and hold it to temperature. A wrap of asbestos paper around the side of the can will help to maintain wax temperature by reducing heat loss.

Candle dipping (Courtesy George Arold, Hatfield, Pa.)

To melt slabs or blocks of wax it is best to break or cut them into pieces. The pieces of wax are placed into the can and melted to provide a depth of wax sufficient for the length of candle to be made. It is suggested that the depth of melted wax be about one inch greater than the length of candle to be made.

Fully refined highly normal paraffin wax with an oil content less than 0.5 percent and a melting point between 130° and 145° F. is preferred for use in making dipped candles. Two such waxes have properties as shown in Table No. 16.

Smaller size plaited or braided wicks are generally best for use in making tapers with a base diameter up to about one inch. Among these are the 6/0 and the 6/0TT square-braided wick and the 15-ply-plaited wick. For best performance of a candle with a given average diameter, the wick size should be balanced against melting point of the wax used. If a candle is to be dripless the 6/0TT square braided wick with wax E is recommended. If an "arty" dripping type candle is to be made, the 15-ply-plaited wick with a 120° to 125° F. melting point wax is suggested. The plaited wick hooks in the flame area, which puts the flame off center and weakens one side of the candle. With low-melting-point wax an excess is melted by the flame to run down the weak side of the candle.

Table No. 16

DIP CANDLE WAXES

	Wax D	Wax E
Melting Point, D-87, °F.	131	140
Congealing Point, D-938, °F.	131	141
Oil Content, D-721, %	0.4	0.2
Pen. Hardness, D-1321, 0.1mm		
at 77°F.	10	7
100°	45	13
110°	103	23
120°	188	92
Kinematic Viscosity, D-445, cs.		
at 160°	5.8	6.8
180°	4.5	5.5
210°	3.5	4.1
Hydrocarbon Type, by Mol. Sieve[1]		
% Normal Paraffins	97	95
% Non-Normals	3	5
Carbon No. Distribution, by G.C.[2]		
Hydrocarbon Range	C 19–33	C 22–35
Peak Point, and %	C 25, 17%	C 29, 19%

[1] Molecular Sieve Analysis
[2] Gas Chromatography Analysis

Candle dipping wheel (Courtesy George Arold, Hatfield, Pa.)

Having chosen the wax and wick combination to be used, the wicking is cut to suitable lengths and arranged for dipping. Each length of wicking is tied at one end to a stick or dowel and spaced apart about twice the thickness of the candle to be made. A small nut or washer is tied to the lower end of each length of wicking to weight it and hold it straight.

A candle is built up layer by layer on each length of wicking by repeated dipping into wax at controlled temperature in an established cycle. It is important that conditions be controlled for production of best appearing candles. Conditions should be such as to give good layer adhesion and a smooth surface, with a reasonable rate of candle build up per dip. If the wax temperature is too low and the dip time too short, layer adhesion will be poor and the surface will be rough and bumpy. If the wax temperature is higher than need be and the dip time is too long, the layers will be thin and production time will be long. Air temperature influences cooling rate between dips.

Accordingly, with a 130° F. melting point wax (having physical properties similar to Wax D), and with air temperature at about 75° F., optimized candle production is obtained with the wax at

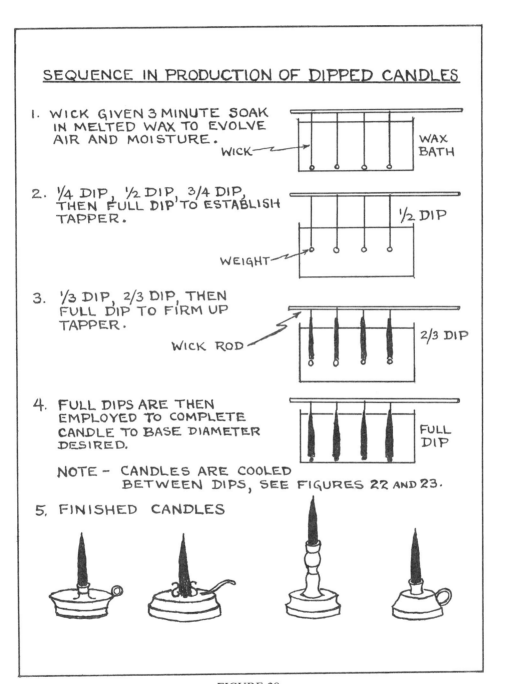

SEQUENCE IN PRODUCTION OF DIPPED CANDLES

1. WICK GIVEN 3 MINUTE SOAK IN MELTED WAX TO EVOLVE AIR AND MOISTURE.

   WICK

   WAX BATH

2. 1/4 DIP, 1/2 DIP, 3/4 DIP, THEN FULL DIP TO ESTABLISH TAPPER.

   1/2 DIP

   WEIGHT

3. 1/3 DIP, 2/3 DIP, THEN FULL DIP TO FIRM UP TAPPER.

   WICK ROD

   2/3 DIP

4. FULL DIPS ARE THEN EMPLOYED TO COMPLETE CANDLE TO BASE DIAMETER DESIRED.

   FULL DIP

   NOTE - CANDLES ARE COOLED BETWEEN DIPS, SEE FIGURES 22 AND 23.

5. FINISHED CANDLES

FIGURE 28

a temperature 160° F. and a 3 to 5 second dip, with 2 to 3 minutes between each dip.

To insure a smooth candle the wick is first given a 3-minute soak in the melted wax to evolve air and moisture. The prewaxed wick is then smoothed between the fingers as it is allowed to cool. A rough bubbly surface is thereby avoided, upon which the candle is built.

To establish a taper, partial dips may be used at first. For example, dip one quarter of the way into the wax, then one half, three quarters, and finally a full dip. This may then be followed by a one-third dip, then a two-thirds dip, with full dips being used to complete the candle to the base diameter desired. This sequence is shown in Figure 28.

Stearic acid, at a concentration of 10 to 20 percent, has in the past been used in dipped candle wax to contribute an opaque appearance. It may presently be replaced with 0.5 to 1.0 percent of Elvax 210 to achieve the same appearance and candle quality. Influence of production conditions upon production rate and candle quality may be illustrated in dipped candles made with Wax D containing 0.5 percent Elvax 210. In all instances 60 gram, 12-inch-long tapers having a 0.85-inch base diameter were produced. In using a 3-second dip time, Figure 29 shows that as wax temperature is increased the number of dips required increases, with a cycle time between 2 and 5 minutes. Accordingly this unnecessarily lengthens production time. Figure 30 shows that in using a 5-second or a 10-second dip time with wax at 160° F., there is very little difference in the number of dips required when 3- to 5-minute cycles are used. It is only at the 2-minute cycle that the 10-second dip time is seen to necessitate a greater number of dips than when a 5-second dip is employed.

For practical production of dipped candles, conditions should be employed that allow production of best appearing candles with the least number of dips. In general this is achieved with wax temperature at about 30° F. above the melting point of the wax, with dip times adjusted accordingly as indicated in the charts.

Air temperature and drafts may markedly affect production rate as well as appearance of dipped candles. With a draft of cooled air, dipped candles tend to bow inward on the side struck by it. This type of bowing may be avoided by rotating the rod holding the candles 180 degrees between each dip. If room temperature is high, cooling rate of the dipped candle is reduced. Not only is production

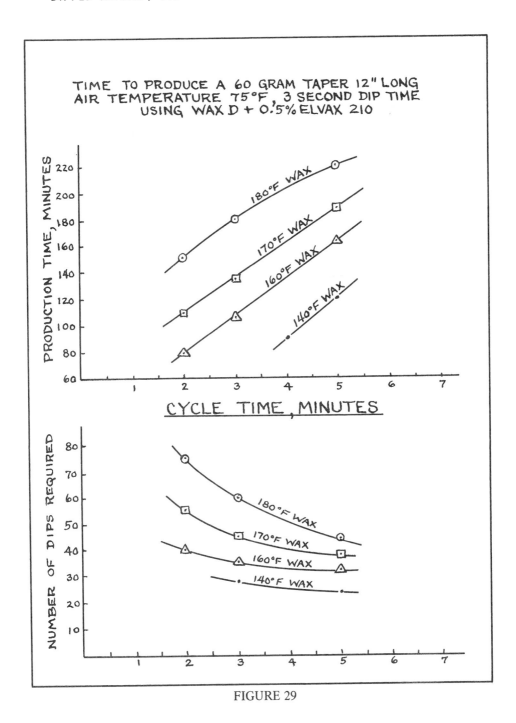

FIGURE 29

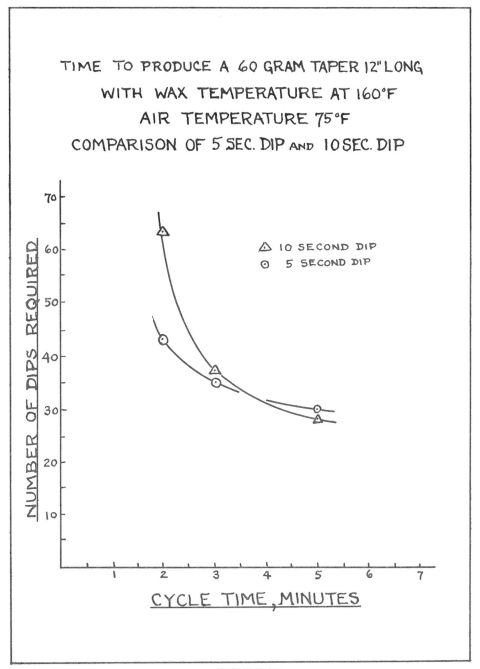

FIGURE 30

time lengthened by a high atmospheric temperature, candle appearance may also be affected. The candle may lose whiteness, tend toward translucency, and acquire a roughened surface. High room temperatures may be compensated for by reducing wax temperature and lengthening the cooling time between dips. For example, with Wax D containing 0.5 percent Elvax 210, a very white, smooth, opaque, satin-finish candle is produced when air temperature is above 80° F., by dropping the wax temperature to 140° F. (rather than 160° F.) and at the same time lengthening the cooling period between dips from 2 minutes to 5 minutes, using a 5-second dip. This is summarized in the following Table No. 17.

Table No. 17

PRODUCTION OF DIPPED CANDLES WITH WAX D + 0.5% ELVAX 210
Using 6/0 Square Braided Wick, Air Temperature 82°F.

Dipping Conditions			Production Rate (60 gram 12 inch candle)		Candle Appearance
Wax Temp.	Cycle Time	Dip Time	No. of Dips	Total Time	
160°F.	2 min.	5 sec.	47	94 min.	Translucent, very smooth
142°F.	5 min.	5 sec.	24	120 min.	Very white, opaque, satin finish, and smooth

The influence of production conditions upon dipped candle appearance is further summarized in Table No. 18 on page 108.

Wick type and size influence burning rate—the larger the wick, the higher the burning rate. This is shown with tapers made with Wax D containing 0.5 percent Elvax 210 as follows:

Burning Rate, grams per hour
12-inch-long tapers, 0.85-inch base diameter[3]

Wick in Decreasing Size	Burning Rate During 8 hours
15 ply, flat plaited	6.4
5/0 square braided	6.1
6/0 square braided	5.9
6/0TT square braided	5.0

[3] Candles made with wax at 170°F. in a 3-second dip and a 2-minute cycle.

By using Wax E containing 0.5 percent Elvax 210 (140° F.

Table No. 18

WAX D + 0.5 PERCENT ELVAX 210 AT 160°F., 2 MIN. CYCLE, 5 SEC. DIP

Candles made using 15 ply wick, with dips and touches[4]

Room Air Conditions	Production of 60 gm, 12" Taper			Candle Appearance		Wax Appearance
	#Dips	Time, Mins.	Taper	Smoothness	Straightness	
64°F., circulating air	26	52	good	mod. bumpy	tends to bow[5]	very white
75°F., no drafts	43	86	good	smooth	straight no bow	very white
84°F., no drafts	46	92	good	very bumpy	straight no bow	very white
80°F. (insulated box) reduced cooling rate	49	98	good	very bumpy	straight no bow	translucent

[4] Wick given 3-minute presoak in wax and allowed to harden before actual dipping. Number of dips include: 2 full dips, 4 touches (i.e. ¼, ½, ¾, full dip), full dip, 3 touches (i.e. ⅓, ⅔, full dip); then full dips to produce a 60 gm, 12" candle.

[5] Bowing tends to occur on the side toward the cool air draft. Bowing may be corrected by rotating candles 180° with respect to the direction of the draft after each dip.

Note: A cold air draft tends to form blisters on the rapidly cooled side of straight wax candles or candles containing stearic acid. Cold air drafts on dipped candles during production should be avoided.

M.P.) in place of Wax D containing 0.5 percent Elvax 210 (130° F. M.P.), candle burning rate is reduced with any one wick size. For example, in candles made with these two waxes and using the 6/0TT and the 6/0 square-braided wick, burning rates and candle performances were obtained as shown in Table No. 19.

To summarize burning data indicate:

1. With each wick size, an increase in wax melting point decreases burning rate.

2. With each candle wax, burning rate is increased with increase in wick size. This may be expected.

3. In most instances, with candles having the same wicking, the presence of as little as 0.5 percent Elvax 210 decreases burning rate and dripping. As might be expected, the presence of Elvax 210 decreases capillarity of the melted wax by contributing slight wick plugging, which in turn reduces burning rate.

4. In regard to candle dripping, sometimes called guttering, indications are that it may result from use of a wick that is too small for the wax being burned. That is to say, the burning rate is too slow for the rate at which the wax is being melted. The 6/0 square-braided wick appears to be optimum for Wax D or Wax E containing 0.5 percent Elvax 210. These candles burn with a preferred essentially dry socket.

As previously discussed in Chapter 5 on additives, it is strongly suggested that as little as 0.5 percent to 1.0 percent Elvax 210 be used in dipped candle wax to replace stearic acid customarily used. By this means a good performing candle may be made at a material cost savings.

Table No. 19

BURNING QUALITY, DIPPED TAPERS

12"-long, 0.85" base diam., burned 8 hours

Wax	6/0TT Sq.-Braided Wick		6/0 Sq.-Braided Wick	
	Burn. Rate, gms/Hr.	gms Drip	Burn Rate, gms/Hr.	gms Drip
Wax D, Blank	5.0	1.8	6.1	0.3
Wax D + 0.5% Elv. 210	5.0	None	5.9	None
Wax E, Blank	4.7	0.6	5.4	0.2
Wax E + 0.5% Elv. 210	4.2	0.3	5.3	None

9
Molded Candles

Molded candles are another interesting variety of candles that are made commercially, among which many varieties may be made at home. They may be made in an almost infinite variety of sizes and shapes, some of which are shown in Figure 31. They may be mass produced in automated or semi-automated machines. Individual and unique molds are used in home crafting of molded candles. Molds are made of any type of material from which the solidified candle may be removed.

Machine-molded candles probably represent the largest volume of commercial candles produced for home use. They are generally made by solidifying melted wax in water cooled metal molds. In a recent development, molded candles are also produced by compression molding of powdered wax. Mass-produced machine-molded candles made from melted wax are for the most part cylindrical, tapered, or spiral shaped. Home-crafted molded candles made from melted wax have almost no limit as to size or shape—only the ingenuity of the home craftsman. As might be expected, each type of molded candle may present special problems, which are to be resolved to produce trouble-free mold release of best appearing and best performing candles. It is these points that are to be discussed in this chapter to guide both the home craftsman and the commercial candle manufacturer.

Candles molded in glass to be burned there without release from the mold are not included in this discussion. This type of candle has been discussed in Chapter 7 on Jar-Lites. However, wick-area conical contraction, as pointed out in discussing Jar-Lites, is an equally pertinent problem in solidifying melted wax in candle molds.

110

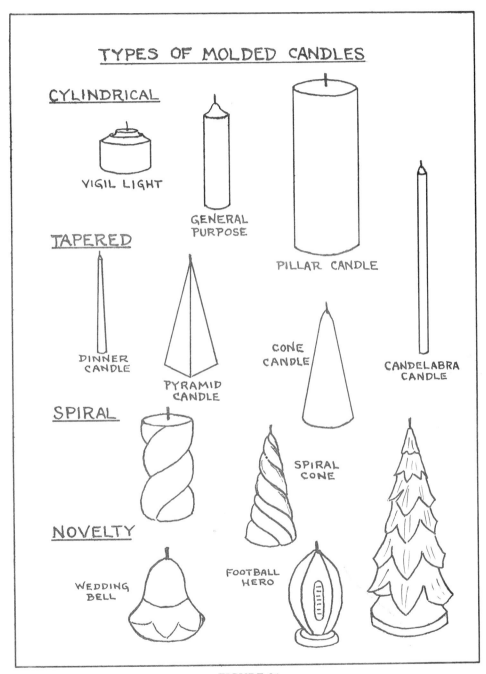

FIGURE 31

Colonial Tinned Candle Mold (Courtesy George Arold, Hatfield, Pa.)

"Pipe-organ" candle mold (Courtesy George Arold, Hatfield, Pa.)

Colonial Tinned Candle Mold (Courtesy George Arold, Hatfield, Pa.)

In making molded candles they should have good mold release, excellent conformity to the mold surface should be allowed, and the finished candle should have a smooth uniform appearance. These factors in producing molded candles are dependent upon several variables, including the material of which the mold is made, shape and smoothness of the molding surface, type of wax used, mold and wax temperatures when the wax is poured, and the rate at which the wax is cooled. These factors are to be considered in some detail.

Machine-Molded Candles Using Melted Wax

In machine molding of candles using melted wax, the molds are water jacketed and contain an internal piston that ejects the candle when it has solidified. There are two types of machine-operated molds. In one type, the wick is present in the mold when the wax is poured into it. In the second type, there is a metal pin in the center of the mold, which casts a hole in the center of the molded candle to accommodate the wick in a second operation. However, it is generally preferred to have the wick present when the candle is molded to eliminate the secondary handling required to wick the candle. Both types of molded candles are to be considered in the following discussion. While practices may be suggested for one type of production, many are also applicable to all others. It is therefore suggested that, for a full appreciation of best techniques for production, the reader become familiar with the subject matter in the entire chapter.

Prewaxed, flat-plaited wicking or square-braided wicking is used when candles are molded with the wick in place. A general discussion on candle wicking is given in Chapter 5. The size wick selected for use is dependent upon melting point of the wax, diameter of the candle to be made, and candle burning performance required. Examples of wicking for given type candles will be discussed later in this chapter. In operating the molding machine, wick is fed to each mold from a separate bobbin located below each mold. It is fed up through the hollow piston rod into the center of each mold, then tied off to a rod across the top. This is shown in Figure 32.

There are precautions that should be observed in adjusting the wick. It is important that it is centered and the tension be just taut. If the wick is off center the candle will not burn evenly. If the wick

MACHINE MOLDING OF CANDLES
WITH WICKING IN PLACE

STEP ONE –
WICKING IS CENTERED IN MOLDS. PISTON IS PUT
IN THE DOWN POSITION.

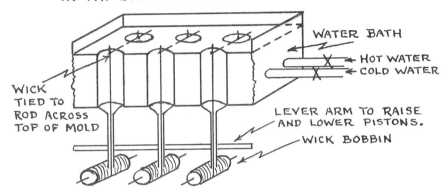

WATER BATH

HOT WATER
COLD WATER

WICK
TIED TO
ROD ACROSS
TOP OF MOLD

LEVER ARM TO RAISE
AND LOWER PISTONS.

WICK BOBBIN

STEP TWO –
WAX POURED INTO WARMED MOLDS SUFFICIENT TO
FLOOD TABLE ABOVE THE MOLDS. COLD WATER
INTRODUCED INTO BATH TO SOLIDIFY CANDLES.

STEP THREE –
WHEN CANDLES ARE COMPLETELY SOLIDIFIED
EXCESS WAX IS SCRAPED FROM TABLE. CANDLES
ARE EJECTED FROM MOLDS BY RAISING PISTON
WHICH PULLS WICKING UP INTO PLACE FOR
NEXT SET OF CANDLES.

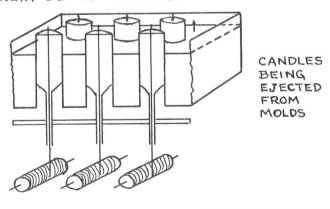

CANDLES
BEING
EJECTED
FROM
MOLDS

FIGURE 32

Bank of candle molds, with pistons down and wick pins up (Courtesy National Candle Co., New York)

is under excessive tension it is stretched to smaller size, which will give a lower burning rate than that size wick would normally provide.

With the wick properly in place, and the piston in the down position, as shown in Figure 32, the mold temperature is adjusted by circulating water of proper temperature through the jacket. Melted wax at controlled temperature is then poured into the mold to solidify. It is important that the cooling rate be controlled to obtain best appearance and best mold release of the solidified candle. Rate of cooling is controlled by temperature of the mold and temperature of the wax when it is poured, as well as temperature adjustment of jacket water during the cooling period.

Good conformation of the wax to the molding surface should be provided for by an adequate mold temperature and wax pouring temperature. Mold and wax temperatures should be high enough to allow release of air bubbles before the wax solidifies, and to avoid rings and ripples that form against excessively cold mold surfaces. These degrade candle appearance. Wax pouring temperature and candle cooling rate also influence mold release, candle structure, and strength characteristics. These properties are also influenced by candle wax composition.

For best operating conditions it is suggested that mold temperature be slightly above room temperature (i.e., 70 to 80° F.) when the wax is poured. With some waxes it may be helpful to drain the

Bank of candle molds with liquid wax flowing over surface to fill the molds (Courtesy National Candle Co., New York)

water from the mold jacket before the wax is poured. Wax temperature should be approximately 30 to 35° F. above the melting point of the wax when it is poured into the mold. The molds should be completely filled with melted wax and there should be an excess of wax in the reservoir chamber above each mold. Approximately ten minutes time is allowed for escape of air bubbles before the jacket water is reintroduced or cooled. Jacket water temperature should then be gradually reduced to about 50° F. Candles should not be shock chilled during initial molding, but may be rapidly chilled after the wax has cooled to about 25° F. below its melting point. Contraction of wax down into the molds is provided for by the excess of wax above each mold.

Bank of candle molds, filled with liquid wax starting to solidify (white film is solidified wax) (Courtesy National Candle Co., New York)

If properties and characteristics of the wax being used are un-known, cooling rate for best mold release and candle appearance should be determined experimentally with the size candle being produced. Most often cooling rate should be optimized between the two extremes of too rapid and too slow. A close cut highly normal paraffin wax may crack in shock chilling, while a broad spectrum highly isoparaffinic wax may bond to the mold giving difficult mold release. Both cracking and sticking situations obviously reduce pro-duction rate and should be avoided. Excessively slow cooling of a close cut highly normal paraffin wax produces a snow spotted poor structured candle. This degrades appearance and strength charac-teristics of the candle. With waxes that may only be slow cooled to

Solid candles forced from molds by cranking pistons up with large wheel at front of machine (Courtesy National Candle Co., New York)

obtain good release, poor structure may be corrected by adjusting wax composition. This is accomplished by blending two or more melting point grades to broaden the wax spectrum, or by adding 1 percent of a 170° F. melting point microwax, or 10 percent of a 150° F. melting point semi-microwax. Addition of up to 1 percent of a low molecular weight polyethylene, for example AC-6, may also be used as an effective route to improve candle wax appearance and strength characteristics.

While a high melt index Ethylene-Vinyl Acetate copolymer may be used to improve candle wax structure, its use in machine-molded candles has the disadvantage in that it may aggravate mold sticking. When mold sticking is a problem there are mold release agents that may be used, including a silicone spray or a white oil wipe on the mold surface. In some instances addition of up to 20 percent stearic acid to the candle wax aids mold release. These candles, sometimes known as stearine candles, have an opaque, satin-like appearance, which may be an added advantage.

Waxes suggested for use in production of machine-molded candles include those shown in Table No. 20. All handle well under controlled molding conditions.

Table No. 20

PHYSICAL PROPERTIES OF PETROLEUM WAXES RECOMMENDED FOR USE IN PISTON-TYPE MACHINES FOR MOLDING CANDLES WITH PLAITED OR BRAIDED WICKING[1]

	Wax F	Blend G	Blend I
Melting Point, D–87, °F.	150	135	146
Oil Content, D–721, %	0.4	0.6	0.5
Pen. Hardness, D–1321, 0.1mm			
at 77°F.	8	9	9
100°F.	13	25	17
110°F.	18	82	22
Kinematic Viscosity, D–445, cs			
at 160°F.	10.9	6.6	8.9
180°F.	7.0	4.9	6.3
210°F.	5.1	3.7	4.7

[1] Including Wax D and Wax E shown in Table No. 2, Chapter 4.

In somewhat more detail on machine-molded candles, the candle wax shrinks down from the reservoir area into the mold as the candle is cooled to solidify. It is for this reason that excess wax is charged to the reservoir above each mold. Upon complete solidification of the candles, the rods, to which each wick was tied on the upper part of each mold, are removed and then excess wax is cut away flush and level across the open surface of each mold. The molded candles are now ready to be ejected from the mold by raising the piston in each. With the piston raised, the candle is pulled away from the seat of the piston, which pulls additional wicking through its shaft. The wicking is then cut about ½ inch below the candle thereby freeing the molded candle. With this completed for each candle in the set, the pistons are lowered again and the molds are again readied for the next set of candles to be molded as previously described. Note, the candles are molded upside down, thus the seat of the piston is the top of the finished candle. All of these steps are shown in Figure 32 on page 115.

Materials of construction from which production molds may be made should be considered. Cast aluminum, black iron, or steel are most suitable. To aid mold release of the solidified candle, the inner mold surface should be precision machined, preferably with a slight outward taper. Black iron and steel molds perform best when the molding surface is tin plated and polished. Aluminum has the advantage of providing best heat transfer between the cooling water and the wax. However, the disadvantage of aluminum is that it is soft and thus easily pitted and scored, which makes candle release difficult. Care should be taken to avoid scoring and scratching the inner mold surface. For this reason pistons should be carefully aligned in the molds. A smooth mold surface imparts a smooth, polished surface to the molded candle. Furthermore, surface irregularities are to be avoided as these areas bind the candle giving mold release problems. Brass is not recommended for candle mold use because it has an oxidizing effect upon the wax, which discolors and gives the wax a burnt odor.

Much that has been stated about candles machine molded with wicks also applies to candles machine molded without wicks. In making the second type of molded candle a metal pin is centered in each mold to provide a hole through the candle into which the wick is inserted in a second operation. When the candle is thoroughly solidified, it is ejected from the mold by raising the piston, which also pushes it off of the pin. A prewaxed metal-core wick is then mechanically inserted through the hole casted in the candle. A metal core wick is used because its rigidity makes this type of wicking operation possible. In this operation a machine-measured length of prewaxed metal core wicking is fed from a bobbin, through

Candle wicking machine (Courtesy National Candle Co., New York)

a prestamped metal-base plate, then up through the hole in the candle. The base plate is crimped around the wick and its bent corners are pressed into the bottom surface of the candle. Wicking extending below the surface of the base plate is cut and bent over against the bottom of the candle, which completes the candle. This operation is then repeated with the next candle in a stop and go procedure, one candle after another.

This secondary wicking operation places specific requirements upon the candle wax. To allow handling, it should not be hard and brittle, nor should it be too soft. If the wax is hard and brittle, the candle may crack or chip when it is fed to the wicking machine or when the wick plate is forced into the bottom of the candle. If the candle wax is too soft it will deform in the wicking operation, or it may lose its shape and block to neighboring candles when stored at an elevated temperature. Capability of the wicking machine limits the size of the candles produced by this method, principally to small and medium-sized vigil lights. The wicking operation is shown in Figure 33 on page 124.

The vigil light, and similar candles of about the same size and type, represent the largest quantity of molded candles that are wicked in a secondary operation. These also include wicked cores that are used in making seven-day votive lights, as previously pointed out in Chapter 7. For this reason and from experience, wax used in producing seven-day votive lights is most satisfactory in producing candles that are wicked in a secondary operation. In this way only one wax is needed for production of most candles made with a metal-core wick, including Jar-Lites and those molded without a wick.

Machine-Molded Candles, Using Powdered Wax

Machine molding of candles, using melted wax, is a semi-automated operation in which there is a waiting period between filling the molds and ejecting the finished candles. Time is required for the wax to solidify. However, use of powdered wax in a compression molding process has the advantage of being completely automated and requiring no cooling time before the candle may be ejected.

Powdered wax with particle size up to that of granulated sugar is produced in a spray tower and fed by gravity to compression molds. When the molds are filled they are closed by a piston; whereupon, the powder is compressed to a cohesive candle. After compression the mold is opened and the candle is ejected. Smooth, trouble-free operation depends for the most part upon using a suitable wax and precision timing the sequence of steps in the operation.

Several designs of compression molding machines are used commercially to produce candles from powdered wax, with diameters up to three and one-half inches. Among these designs there are single mold, dual mold, and multimold models. Some may be of private design, others are commercially available. Single and dual mold candle presses are manufactured by Hans Kuerschner, Machine Manufacturer, Kaldenkirchen, West Germany. A rotary candle press is manufactured by Arthur Weissbach, Machine Manufacturer,

PRODUCTION LINE FOR WICKING PREMOLDED CANDLES

PREWAXED METAL CORE WICK (see FIGURE 20) IS HELD IN WICK HOLE OF PREMOLDED CANDLE BY WICK TAB PRESSED INTO THE BOTTOM OF THE CANDLE.

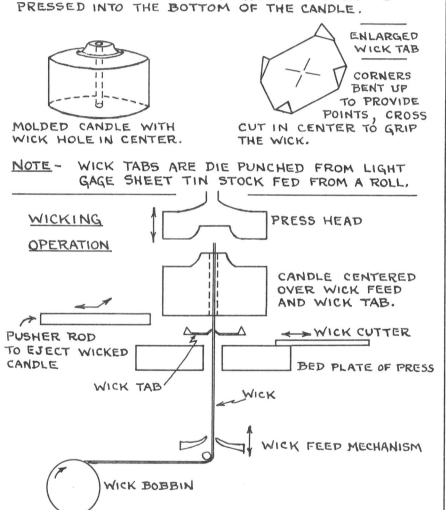

ENLARGED WICK TAB

MOLDED CANDLE WITH WICK HOLE IN CENTER.

CORNERS BENT UP TO PROVIDE POINTS, CROSS CUT IN CENTER TO GRIP THE WICK.

NOTE - WICK TABS ARE DIE PUNCHED FROM LIGHT GAGE SHEET TIN STOCK FED FROM A ROLL.

WICKING OPERATION

PRESS HEAD

CANDLE CENTERED OVER WICK FEED AND WICK TAB.

PUSHER ROD TO EJECT WICKED CANDLE

WICK CUTTER

BED PLATE OF PRESS

WICK TAB

WICK

WICK FEED MECHANISM

WICK BOBBIN

FIGURE 33

Kuerschner Candle Press (Courtesy Jung Atlantic Refining Co., Hamburg, West Germany)

Fulda, West Germany. These machines are finding use in candle manufacturing plants throughout the United States. A possible compression mold design is shown schematically in Figure 34.

While each type of candle press may differ somewhat in design and mechanical detail, all require a free flowing powdered wax as feed for the molds. Powdered wax for compression molding is produced by spraying melted wax into cooled air. For trouble-free performance the powdered wax should be free flowing and should have a particle size distribution that allows air release and good compaction in the mold. If particle size distribution is not controlled, air release tends to be critical in production of candles with a compressed height two and one-half times greater than the diameter.

Particle size distribution is controlled by spray equipment design. Average particle size is controlled by charge temperature of the liquid wax, pressure behind the charge, and spray port design. With properly designed spray equipment a good wax charge temperature is 3 to 5° F. above the melting point of the wax.

The wax is sprayed into the top of an air conditioned accumulation chamber against a slow up-draft of air cooled to about 60° F. To prevent a build-up of static charge on the wax particles, which makes them repel each other, air humidity within the chamber is controlled to about 60 percent of saturation. An excessively damp air should be avoided, as it condenses moist air on the wax particles, which degrades particle cohesion in the compression molding operation. To achieve complete cooling of the wax particles, to avoid agglomeration, and to provide free flow of the powder to the molding equipment, the particle size should not exceed 25 thousandths of an inch in diameter. To avoid build-up of powdered wax in the bottom of the spray tower and prevent compaction under its own weight, powdered wax production should be at a controlled rate, or at controlled intervals. Powdered wax is fed from the bottom of the spray tower, through a trough to the compression molding machines. A "rake" may be rotated in the feed trough to break up agglomerates of powdered wax that may form.

For best performance in compression molding, the paraffin wax should not be tacky but be sufficiently plastic to provide good strength characteristics in the compressed candle and at the same time allow good mold release without sticking. These characteristics are provided in a rather narrow cut 130 to 135° F. melting point wax containing approximately 15 percent non-normal paraffins. A

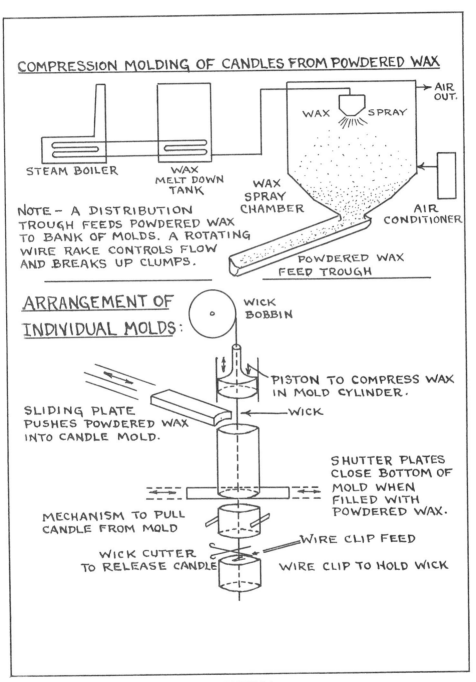

FIGURE 34

broad cut wax with the same melting point and containing more than 20 percent non-normal paraffins would tend to pack as a powder and produce a compressed candle that would tend to stick in the mold. Physical properties of a typical good performing compression molding wax are shown in Table No. 21.

Details on the several types of compression molding equipment do not belong in this discussion. However, a brief description of the Kuerschner Press and the Weissbach Press are described as follows:

Kuerschner Candle Press (Type BP006, MP Model D-23-B).

A self-contained unit capable of compression molding powdered wax into candles up to 3.9 inches in diameter and 11.8 inches tall. Mold diameter and compression stroke may be changed to produce smaller size candles. A single mold press is reported to have the capacity to produce about 100 candles per hour. A dual mold press is capable of making two 2½-inch-diameter candles 9 inches long in one stroke on a six-second cycle. In both models the wick is inserted as the candle is formed.

Weissbach Rotary Press

This equipment produces candles from powdered wax in three stages. In the first stage the mold is filled with powdered wax, in the second the powdered wax is compressed, and in the third the compressed candle is ejected. Each stage is accomplished on a rotating table with one position for each operation.

Table No. 21

PHYSICAL PROPERTIES OF A TYPICAL COMPRESSION MOLDING WAX

Melting Point, D–87, °F.	131
Oil Content, D–721, %	1.0
Refractive Index at 176°F.	1.4290
Penetration Hardness, D–1321	
at 77°F.	13
100°	95
110°	184
Hydrocarbon Type, by Mol. Sieve[2]	
% Normal Par.	85
% Non-Normals	15
Carbon Number Distribution, by M.S.[3]	
Normal Paraffins	85%, C 20–32
Iso-Paraffins	8%, C 28–35
Cyclo-Paraffins	7%, C 27–32

[2] Molecular Sieve Analysis.
[3] Mass Spectra Analysis.

Beehive hollow fluted candles. (*Courtesy Will and Baumer.*)

Privately built compression molding equipment allows variability of design. The equipment may vary from that of a simple pharmaceutical tablet press design to that of a rather sophisticated design. A quotation on fabrication and installation costs of a given type candle press, with a particular design, may be obtained by defining the following requirements in specifications:

1. Size limitations and interchangeability of molds.
2. Maximum compression pressure to be provided by the equipment.
3. Variability of compression cycle time and hold time at maximum pressure.
4. Limitations of equipment in handling particle sizes of wax charge; powder, flakes, chips.
5. The need for spark proof (class D) electrical equipment.
6. Extent of automation required in preparation of wax feed.
7. Extent and type of automation required to operate candle press.
8. Materials of construction should be specified to avoid wear and sticking of vital moving parts. Teflon-coated surfaces are suggested to provide clean mold release of candles.
9. Shape and materials of construction employed in the molds to provide easy release of the molded candles.

Hand-Molded Candles Using Melted Wax

Hand-molded candles, produced by hand pouring melted wax into a prepared mold are particularly well suited to home crafting of candles. Type and shape of mold that may be employed is limited only by imagination. In addition to mold variations, an almost infinite variety of artistic effects may be obtained by colorations and decorations.

A variety of molding materials may be employed. These include cardboard, glass, tin, aluminum, plastic, rubber, and plaster. Polyethylene-coated paper cups and paperboard milk cartons are a convenient form for molding candles. Glass, tin, aluminum, and plastic forms that are open at both ends may also be used. Glass tubing up to about 3 inches inside diameter may be purchased for candle mold use from a laboratory glassware supply house. Tin and aluminum tubes, either square or circular in cross-section, may be purchased from a metals supply shop. Plexiglas tubes are readily available from a plastics supply shop. Any of the tubing may be ordered cut to desired length for candle mold use. To obtain a good seal at the bottom of the mold when it is assembled, it is important that the tubing be cut square and level. A convenient set-up for assembling molds made of tubing is shown in Figure 35. Rubber and plaster molds are related in their use. For convenience, these molding materials will be discussed at the end of this chapter, with specific details given in the Appendix.

Among the many styles of hand-molded candles, the tall pillar type is perhaps the most popular. Depending upon the cross-section shape of the tube used, the candle may be made in a number of shapes including cylindrical, square, star shaped, hexagonal, octagonal and so forth. The sides may be made parallel, tapered to a pyramid, or cone shaped.

In selecting and making a candle mold it is important that release of the candle from the mold be provided for. Both mold material, shape, and assembly should be considered. Paper and paperboard molds as suggested are convenient for one time use. Upon complete solidification of the wax, the paper may be torn and stripped from the candle. Metal, plastic and glass molds intended for reuse should be open at both ends or made in two halves held together with straps. A slight taper from one end to the other is to be preferred in molds that are open at both ends. Light gage metal may be formed to a slight taper. Heavy gage metal or plastic molds may be machined to a taper. This allows release of the candle through the larger opening. Dents and surface imperfections are to be avoided as they are areas where the candle may bind in the mold. The stepwise procedure for assembling the mold shown in Figure 35 is as follows:

A. *Assembly of Mold for Producing Hand Crafted Candles*

    (1) Prewax a suitable length of 2/0 braided, or 15-ply plaited wicking by dipping it into hot wax for 30 seconds. Remove the wick from the wax bath and wipe it with a paper towel to smooth down the fibers, then allow it to cool while holding it straight.

    (2) Thread the stiff wick through the hole in the center of the aluminum foil and gasket, then through the hole in the board. Pull about one inch length of wick through the bottom of the board and fasten it in place with a plug of melted wax that is allowed to solidify.

    (3) Hold the sheet of foil and gasketing against the board in an upside down position with the wick dangling. Place this

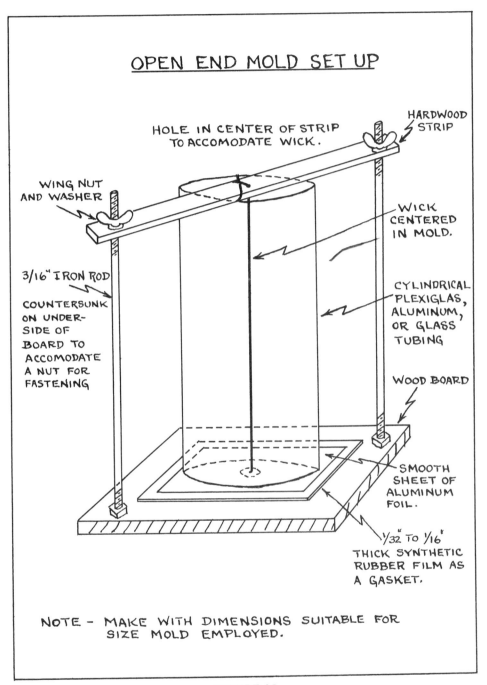

FIGURE 35

assembly down onto the mold with the wick down through the center of the mold. Grab the free end of the wick, turn the mold right side up, and set it down on the wood base.

(4) Thread the free end of the wick through the middle hole in the hardwood strip and place the strip down onto the top of the mold with an iron rod through the hole at each end of the strip.

(5) Center the mold around the wick hole in the wood board and gasketing, making certain that the foil and gasket are flat against the board without wrinkles.

(6) Place a washer and wing nut on each rod and fasten the hardwood strip evenly and firmly onto the top surface of the mold. This fastening transfers mold pressure against the gasket and effectively seals the bottom of the mold.

(7) Pull the wick up snug and centered in the mold and tie it securely onto the cross strip.

The mold is now set up and ready for melted wax to be poured into it to form a candle. But, what molding conditions and which wax should be used? Candle mold release and candle appearance are related to the wax used and the cooling conditions employed, as well as the material of which the mold is made. Air cooling of the wax may be employed where production rate is not of major concern. Cooling with air at a given temperature is slower than cooling with water at the same temperature. The critical conditions previously pointed out in discussing machine molding water-cooled candles are equally pertinent to air cooling hand-molded candles. However, wax composition becomes much more important when candles are air cooled. With slow rate air cooling, a narrow-cut, highly normal paraffin wax tends to form a non-uniform structured candle, with snow spots. A hand-molding wax that solidifies with good structure in air cooling is a broad spectrum wax that contains 8 to 10 percent of non-normal paraffins. This wax may be made by blending 10 percent of a 150° F. melting point semi-microwax into a poor performing 130° F. melting point close-cut, highly normal paraffin wax. Physical properties of the base waxes, Wax D and Wax J, are shown in Table No. 22 along with properties of a 90–10 blend of the two waxes.

Table No. 22

PHYSICAL PROPERTIES OF A CORRECTED WAX
FOR HAND MOLDING OF CANDLES

	Wax D	Wax J	Wax Blend H 10% Wax J 90% Wax D
Melting Point, D–87, °F.	132.6	151.0	133.4
Oil Content, D–721, %	0.3	1.0	0.4
Refractive Index at 176°F.	1.4275	1.4358	1.4286
Penetration Hardness, D–1321			
at 77°F.	6	10	13
100°	40	23	73
110°	90	34	122
Hydrocarbon Type, by Mol. Sieve[4]			
% Normal Par.	97.6	64.2	92
% Non-Normals	2.4	35.8	8
Carbon Number Distribution, by G.C.[5]			
Range	C19 to C33	C22 to C50	C19 to C50
Peak	C25	C33	C34
Appearance in a Slow Cooled Candle	Poor, snow spots	Excellent	Excellent

---

[4] Molecular Sieve Analysis
[5] Gas Chromatographic Analysis

B. *Molding Conditions for Producing Hand Crafted Candles*

  (1) With the candle mold assembled and the wick in place and centered, the wax should be poured into the mold at a high enough temperature to allow good mold conformation and air bubble release before the wax starts to solidify.

  (2) Select a cool environment for the mold assembly. With Wax blend H (melting point about 133° F.) have the wax at 180 to 190° F. and carefully fill the mold to the top with liquid wax.

  (3) Allow the mold and wax to cool about 30 minutes before making a second pour to make up for contraction. After a total cooling period of four hours the candle should be probed with a pointed ⅛"-diameter steel rod. The candle should be probed in the wick area to expose any hidden cavities that may have formed while the wax was cooling. At least three holes should be probed to a depth of at least several inches. The holes and any cavities that may have been uncovered are then filled with the wax at a temperature of 160° F.

(4) The candle is then allowed to cool completely, about eight hours at 72° F. room temperature. The mold is released from the rack by removing the wing bolts and untying the wick from the cross bar. The gasket and the aluminum foil are then removed from what is to be the top of the finished candle.

(5) The opposite end of the mold, being the top of the mold in the rack, is then sharply tapped onto a solid wood surface to break the candle loose. If difficulty is encountered in releasing the candle from the mold, both may be placed into a refrigerator or cold water bath to shrink the candle. With the candle loosened in the mold it is then pushed out. Note, use of a tapered mold will reduce sticking of the candle in the mold. If used it should be placed in the rack with the narrow dimension down. It is then pushed out of the mold through the wide upper end. A thin film of white oil may be used as a mold release agent on the inner surface of a Plexiglas mold. If a glass mold is used a thin film of silicone oil may be applied.

(6) With the candle out of the mold, the end that was against the aluminum foil is smooth and flat, the other end is to be flattened and leveled. This is accomplished by use of a sharp knife or by briefly standing the bottom of the candle on a level surfaced hotplate.

(7) If need be, the candle surface may be polished by rubbing it with a soft cloth or nylon stocking.

Artistic Types of Molded Candles Using Melted Wax

A chapter on molded candles would not be complete without at least mentioning some of the many artistic types of molded candles. Many candle hobbyists find fancy molded candles to be their greatest interest. They are particularly well suited to originality in hand molding and finishing. A list of artistic types of molded candles, though it may not be complete, may serve to stimulate the imagination to invent an original variety of molded candle.

Included among fancy, artistic, molded candles are:

1. Pillar candles that when burned form petals of unconsumed wax. These candles are known as foliating type or angel wing type.
2. Candles that are crackled or marbleized in appearance.

3. Candles that are laced with holes for an artistic effect.
4. Candles that are made up of concentric or horizontal layers of contrasting colors.
5. Candles decorated on the surface with foamed wax.
6. Decorative candle shells that are filled with foamed wax.
7. Flower petal candles that may be floated on water, as for example water lilies.
8. Figurines, cut-glass objects, and ceramic art objects reproduced as candles.

A brief discussion of these artistic type candles may be helpful to the home candle craftsman.

Petal forming candles, known in the trade as foliating or angel winged candles, perform through selection of the correct wax and wick combination for the candle diameter. Use of an undersized wick relative to the candle diameter allows a wall of unburned wax to form. This may be aided by molding a candle with a dished-in top. When the wall of unburned wax is thin enough and the wax is plastic enough at the temperature produced by the flame, the wall buckles outward, splits down from its own weight, and starts

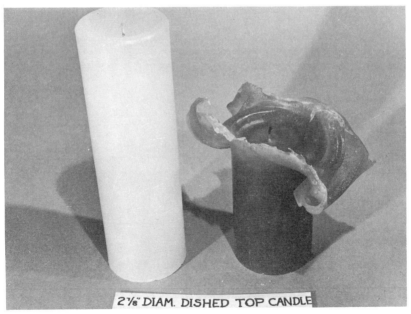

Candle molded with dished in top to stimulate foliation (Courtesy Atlantic Richfield Co., Phila., Pa.)

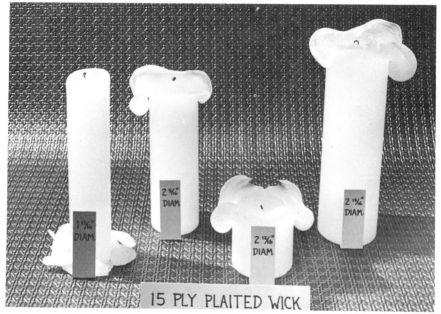

Candle foliation related to candle diameter (Courtesy Atlantic Richfield Co., Phila., Pa.)

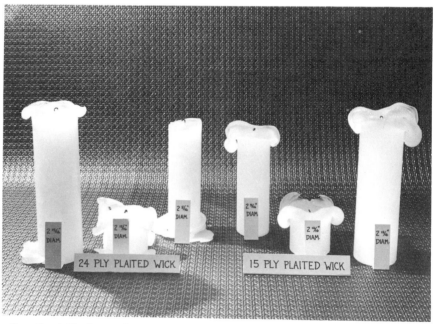

Candle foliation related to wick size and candle diameter (Courtesy Atlantic Richfield Co., Phila., Pa.)

the petal formation. When burned periodically, for example three hours at a time, attractive ripples form on the petals.

Wax Blend H, recommended for use in producing hand-molded candles, is suggested for production of 2¾- to 3-inch-diameter foliating candles. When a 15-ply, flat-plaited wick is used, good burning and self-foliation is provided in a 2¾-inch-diameter candle. A 2/0 square braided wick, with a higher burning rate than the 15-ply wick, is suggested for use with a 3-inch-diameter candle made with Wax Blend H. A uniform structured air cooled candle is produced with this wax.

If a snow spotted, arty appearing, air cooled candle is preferred, a wax blend comprising 60 percent 132° F. melting-point wax and 40 percent 140° F. melting-point wax is suggested. Physical properties of the two components and the 60–40 blend are given in Table No. 23.

Table No. 23

PHYSICAL PROPERTIES OF COMPONENTS AND WAX BLEND
FOR PRODUCTION OF SNOW SPOTTED SELF-FOLIATING CANDLES

	Wax D	Wax E	Wax Blend G 60% Wax D 40% Wax E
Melting Point, D–87, °F.	132.6	140.4	135.2
Oil Content, D–721, %	0.3	0.2	0.3
Refractive Index at 176°F.	1.4275	1.4300	1.4285
Penetration Hardness, D–1321			
at 77°F.	6	7	9
100°	40	13	25
110°	90	23	82
Hydrocarbon Type, by Mol. Sieve[6]			
% Normal Par.	97.6	95.6	96.5
% Non-Normals	2.4	4.4	3.5
Carbon Number Distribution, by G.C.[7]			
Range	C19 to C23	C22 to C35	C19 to C35
Peak	C25	C29	C27
Appearance in a Slow Cooled Candle	Snow Spots	Slight Snow	Snow Spots

[6] Molecular Sieve Analysis
[7] Gas Chromatographic Analysis

These candles are made as described under hand-molded candles using melted wax.

Marbleized appearance is produced by shock chilling a candle after it has been removed from the mold. To obtain a good appearing marbleized effect the candle should be made of a suitably structured wax. Blend H Wax, suggested for production of self-foliating candles, has the type of structure best suited. A large diameter candle is suggested. It is crackled by shock chilling in water 30° F. below candle temperature for two minutes. Permanence of the crackle is enhanced by having the candle at about 85° F. and quenching in 55° F. water. By crackling a large diameter foliating candle in cold water the ability of the candle to self-foliate is not degraded.

Multicolored candles may be made in several ways. Chunks of varied colored high melting wax may be packed into a mold, after which the voids are filled with a lower melting white wax. A variety of colored waxes may be consecutively poured into a mold and solidified in a cross-sectional or horizontal layer pattern, one layer at a time. Another method would be to cast a candle of one colored wax, then dip coat to apply layers of contrasting colored waxes, one layer after another. These methods are briefly detailed as follows:

1. Colored wax chunks may be produced by casting a pan full of each colored wax, then when fully solidified either cut each color into pieces or break it into pieces for use. Wax J suggested as a blend component for foliating type candles may be used to produce the colored wax chunks. A quantity of this wax is melted and a different wax-soluble dye dissolved in each of several portions.

In making up the candle, a mold as shown in Figure 35 may be used. Wax D, suggested as the second component for producing foliating candles, may be used as the fill wax. In making a 2¾- to 3-inch-diameter candle, a 2/0 square-braided wick may be used. With the mold set up and the wick in place, it is suggested that the mold be partially filled with undyed Wax D at about 140° F. Cold chunks of colored wax are then dropped into the mold to fill it the desired amount. The mold and the fill wax are then rapidly cooled to solidify the variegated colored candle. Upon release from the mold, the top of the candle as oriented in the mold is trimmed and leveled. Experimentation may be required to develop the best technique for producing this type of variegated candle.

2. Colored waxes in horizontal layers in the candle are produced by pouring a depth of one colored wax at a time into the mold. When solidified, the next layer of another colored wax is poured and so forth.

3. Colored waxes in concentric rings in the candle may be produced in one of two ways. In one way the mold is filled with a wax of one color and allowed to solidify in a cooled atmosphere just long enough to form a shell of solidified wax against the mold wall and the bottom of the mold, with the center still fluid. When a wall of solidified wax of sufficient thickness has formed, the unsolidified wax in the center is poured out. A skin of solidified wax across the top surface may have to be broken to allow this. The void in the center of the candle is then filled with wax of another color. The other way of producing a concentric ring candle, with each ring a different color, is to cast a candle of one color then dip it into the other colored waxes. Each layer is applied one at a time, allowing complete solidification before the next dip is made. This operation is repeated until the full diameter candle is made.

Candles laced with holes are produced by loosely packing small ice cubes into the candle mold before the wax is poured. When the wax has completely solidified, the candle is removed. The ice is then allowed to melt and drain from the candle. A continuous one piece candle laced with holes will result if the ice had been packed loose enough in the mold. Note: To avoid a water-soaked wick, which would cause burning failure, a heavily waxed and smoothed wick should be employed in making up the mold.

Shell Candles made of a high-melting wax are filled with a foamed low-melting-point wax so that the shell can act as a mantle when the foamed wax is burned. The shell is made as in making the shell for a candle with concentric layers of colored wax. Wax J or Wax E, previously referred to, in which about 2 percent AC-6 polyethylene is dissolved, produces a fine structured wax for the shell. The wax may be dyed to produce a colorful effect as a translucent mantle. The high-melting-point wax is poured into the mold and allowed to solidify to a sufficient thickness on the mold wall and bottom. The top surface skin is then broken and the liquid wax is poured from the center of the mold to produce the shell. If a plaited or braided wick is used it should be in place in the mold when the shell is made. If a metal-core wick is used, it may be put in place after the shell has been made, as when a seven day votive light is produced.

Wax D or Wax A, previously referred to, may be employed to produce foamed wax to fill the shell. The wax is foamed by beating air into it at a temperature just below its melting point. With Wax D a temperature of about 130° F. is suggested, with Wax A a temperature of about 120° F. may be used. With the wax at temperature an electric mixer is employed to beat air into it, being careful not to excessively cool the wax. Having the wick in place, the shell is then quickly filled with foamed wax. This is accomplished by either scooping or pouring the foamed wax into the shell. If a metal-core wick is put in place after the shell has been made, a ½-inch-thick tack pour of foamed wax should first be made to allow the wick to be centered and pulled up taut before the shell is filled with foamed wax. A 6/0 square-braided wick is suggested for use with Wax D. A 34-40 metal-core wick is suggested for use with Wax A.

With the candle fully cooled and solidified it is removed from the mold as in making hand-molded candles using melted wax.

Foamed Wax may be used to decorate a variety of molded candles. To do this a spatula is used to apply the foam to the surface of the candle, much the same as in applying icing to a cake. Artistic decorations may then be pressed into or tucked into the foam while it is warm and soft. Artificial holly leaves and berries may be used on Christmas candles, plastic flowers and petals may be used on party candles, while metallic glitter may be dusted on the foamed wax for a generally decorative candle.

Flower-like candles to be floated on water may be casted in small, petal-shaped molds. Small-size tinned gelatin molds, shallow muffin tins, or specially prepared paper molds supported in a muffin pan may be used. Candles about ½ inch thick are suggested, using Wax D and a 34-40 metal-core wick. The wick should be supported by and crimped into a wick-tin and placed into the center of the mold. It should be long enough to extend at least ⅜ inch above the top surface of the candle.

Art objects reproduced as candles are made by using rigid plaster and flexible rubber casts of the object. Figurines, cut-glass, and ceramic objects may be duplicated by use of these casts, either separately or together, as molds. Plaster is rather inexpensive and easy to use; but, being rigid, its use is restricted principally to rather simple objects. Removal of the plaster cast from the object to be reproduced is aided by making it in two parts. Flexible rubber molds are essential for reproduction of complex figures. A variety of rubbers that cure at room temperature are available for use in producing elastic casts that have excellent strength characteristics.

Among these rubbers are Koroseal FMC and Permaflex CMC supplied by the Permaflex Mold Co. and DPR Flowable Rubber supplied by Hardman, Inc.

The preparation of plaster and flexible rubber casts for use as candle molds is rather involved. For this reason and to provide a general reference, discussion on use of plaster and flexible rubbers is given in the Appendix.

Burning rate data on hand-molded candles made with the several waxes and wicks are given in Tables No. 24 and 25.

Table No. 24

BURNING RATE DATA ON HAND-MOLDED CANDLES

Wax	Wick Type & Size	Candle Diam., Inches	Burn. Rate, Grams/Hr.
C	15-Ply Plaited	2 1/2	5.5*
D	15-Ply Plaited	2 1/2	5.4*
D + 1% AC–6	15-Ply Plaited	2 1/2	5.0*
D + 5% Wax J & 1% AC-6	15-Ply Plaited	2 1/2	4.6*
D	15-Ply Plaited	2 15/16	5.2*
D	30-Ply Plaited	2 15/16	7.6*
D	42-Ply Plaited	2 15/16	8.2*
D	6/0 Sq. Braided	2 15/16	5.0*
D	5/0 Sq. Braided	2 15/16	5.1*
D	2/0 Sq. Braided	2 15/16	7.1*
E	15-Ply Plaited	2 15/16	4.1*
E	30-Ply Plaited	2 15/16	6.9*
E	42-Ply Plaited	2 15/16	7.1*
E	6/0 Sq. Braided	2 15/16	5.1*
E	5/0 Sq. Braided	2 15/16	4.3*
E	2/0 Sq. Braided	2 15/16	7.0*
Wax Blend H	15-Ply Plaited	2 3/4	5.6*
Wax Blend H	15-Ply Plaited	2 3/4	6.2**
Wax Blend H	24-Ply Plaited	2 3/4	6.3*
Wax Blend H	24-Ply Plaited	2 3/4	7.5**
Wax Blend H	36–24 Metal Core	2 3/4	5.0*
Wax Blend H	44–32–18 Metal Core	2 3/4	6.6*

* 3 Hours intermittent burning for a total of 36 hours.
** 24 Hours continuous burning.

Table No. 25

BURNING EVALUATION OF WAX BLEND H CANDLES
Relation of Wick Size to Candle Diameter for Foliation
(3 Hours Intermittent Burning for a total of 36 Hours)

Wick Size and Type	Candle Diam. Inches	Start of Foliation, Hrs.	Quality of Foliation	Wax Drip grams	Burn. Rate grams/Hr.
15-Ply Plaited	2 5/16	20	Excellent	None	5.5
15-Ply Plaited	2 12/16	25	Excellent	None	5.1
15-Ply Plaited	2 15/16	28	Excellent	None	5.3
24-Ply Plaited	2 5/16	—	None	29	6.7
24-Ply Plaited	2 12/16	14 1/2	Good	9	6.5
24-Ply Plaited	2 15/16	14 1/2	Good	30	6.6
6/0TT Braided	1 15/16	11	Good	5	3.9
6/0 Braided	2 5/16	15	Excellent	20	5.1
2/0 Braided	2 15/16	18	Excellent	0	7.1

Note: These data show that burning rate is dependent upon wick size for a given wax used in the candle. Candle performance, including foliation and dripping, is dependent on candle diameter and wick size.

Drilling wick hole in large diameter candle (Courtesy Lumi-craft, Norwick, Ohio)

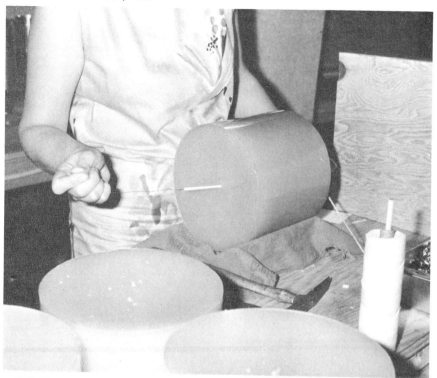

Wicking of drilled candle (Courtesy Lumi-craft, Norwick, Ohio)

Soldering base to candle mold (Courtesy Lumi-craft, Norwick, Ohio)

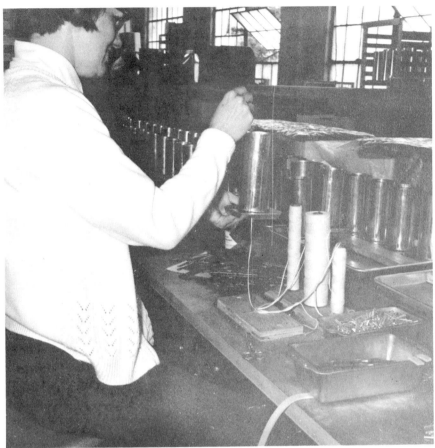

Wicking of candle mold (Courtesy Lumi-craft, Norwick, Ohio)

10
Candles by Extrusion

Extrusion offers the greatest potential for complete automation of candle production. For commercial candle manufacturers an automated extruder is the key to a completely automatic step-wise production of candles, from receipt of wax in bulk, through extrusion, to packaging finished candles.

Several types of extruders have been developed for candle production, including screw type, hydraulic ram type, and rotary drum type. As would be expected, each type of extruder has its own unique characteristics that demand a wax having special properties to obtain best machine performance in production of high quality candles.

A general description of each type extruder is presented to point out the special wax properties that are required for each type of operation.

Candle Production by Screw Extrusion

The three essential parts to a screw extruder are: the wax-feed hopper, the screw and housing, and the die-head. In a sense it is similar to a screw type meat grinder, with exception there is only one hole in the die-head rather than the many holes that are present in a meat grinder.

Wax as chips, flakes, or powder is fed through the hopper into the screw chamber. The rotation of the screw works and compresses the wax to extrude it under pressure through the die as a continuous rod at the exit end of the screw chamber. Wicking from a bobbin is introduced into the chamber through a tube with its

145

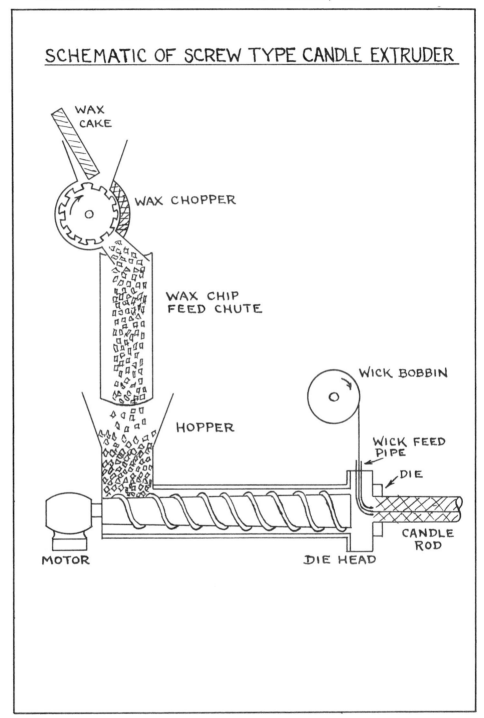

FIGURE 36

outlet centered near the entrance to the die. With the wax in a compressed plastic state at this point, the wick is in effect pulled through by the wax being extruded. A simplified sketch of this equipment is shown in Figure 36.

It is of interest to note that candle extrusion equipment is an adaptation of screw extruders previously employed to extrude plastics, bar-soap, and dough for baked goods. Among the several types of extruders, those that may be employed to extrude wax for production of candles include: the single screw type, the parallel dual screw, the duplex extruder (two single screw extruders connected by a vacuum chamber), and a duplex of two sets of parallel screws.

Precision extrusion of a good appearing continuous candle rod is dependent upon the plastic characteristic of the wax as influenced by temperature. For this reason control of wax temperature in the extrusion chamber is important. This may be accomplished by having a controlled temperature water jacket around the extrusion chamber. Heat produced in working and compressing the wax in the screw chamber is related to the character of the wax and the work done by the screw on the wax. A deep-flighted screw produces less heat than a shallow-flighted screw. Work and extrusion rate are set by the type of screw employed and its rate of rotation. These are not easily changed to accommodate variability among waxes. Thus, for a given extruder, several types of paraffin wax may be accommodated by precise temperature control maintained by regulating the jacket water temperature. In this way optimum operating conditions may be established for a given wax in a particular extruder. When processed through the barrel of the extruder, the wax should be held in the plastic state that usually occurs 20 to 30° F. below its melting point.

A single screw extruder is usually adequate for extruding candles when flakes of wax are used as charge. However, a duplex extruder provides several advantages that are not possible with the single screw extruder. In a duplex, the first screw may be used to blend candle wax components including two or more waxes along with stearic acid and dye. The second stage receives the premixed blend, mixes it some more, and extrudes a candle rod of uniform composition. Temperature and compression control are usually easier to maintain in a duplex extruder than in a single screw extruder. A duplex extruder is usually equipped with a vacuum chamber where air bubbles may be eliminated from the candle wax. Thus, the extruded candle rod would have fewer air bubbles than the rod extruded from a single screw extruder. Occluded air bubbles are to be avoided as they may lead to uneven expansion of the candle when it is stored or possibly a sudden expansion when the candle is burned. Last—but not least—of all, a duplex extruder produces a candle with greater density and strength characteristics than a candle produced from the same wax in a single screw extruder. For these reasons, a duplex screw extruder is to be preferred over a single extruder for production of candles.

The horsepower required to operate an extruder is dependent upon the weight of candle rod produced per unit of time. This is related to production rate of unit candles and diameter of the candle being produced. The lower the production rate, the less horsepower required. To produce 1000 pounds of candles per hour in a duplex extruder, a minimum force of 12 horsepower transmitted to each duplex screw is required. However, reserve horsepower above the minimum required is suggested as being highly desirable.

Most screw extruders designed for candle production are manufactured in Europe. The Steinfels-Mazzoni extruder and the Weber and Seeländer extruder are reported to be the two most popular designs. A sketch of the Weber and Seeländer equipment is shown in Figure 37. In this equipment melted candle wax is continuously charged to the wax pan in which a water-cooled drum is rotated. A wax film of controlled thickness is formed and solidified on the surface of the drum. By means of a doctor blade the solidified wax is removed from the surface of the drum and fed as a ribbon into the hopper of the extruder. The wax feed is worked and compressed in the extruder chamber where it is then forced against the exit die to continuously extrude a wicked candle rod. As the rod is extruded it is cut into desired lengths and trimmed to form a tip and expose the wick. The finished candles are then individually wrapped in paper for distribution. Physical properties of two waxes reported to give excellent performance in a Weber and Seeländer candle extruder are shown in Table No. 26 on page 151.

Change in penetration hardness, with change in temperature as a measure of plasticity by the ASTM, D–1321, Test Method, is a most significant measure of wax suitability for extrusion. Change in hardness with temperature for the two waxes, Wax I and Wax J, is presented graphically in Figure 38. A wax with hardness values within the limits of these two waxes would be expected to give excellent performance in the Weber and Seeländer equipment.

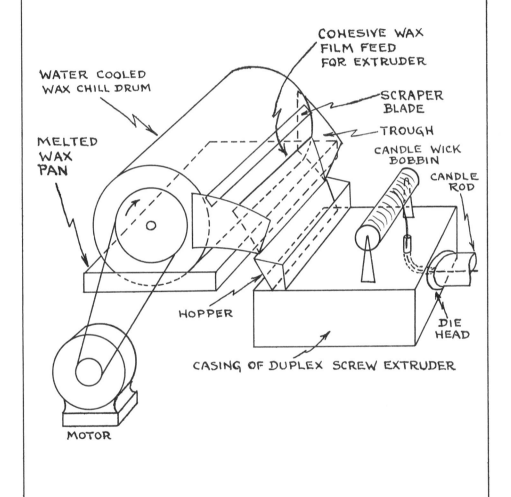

SCHEMATIC OF THE WEBER and SEELÄNDER
SCREW TYPE CANDLE EXTRUDER

COHESIVE WAX FILM FEED FOR EXTRUDER

WATER COOLED WAX CHILL DRUM

SCRAPER BLADE

TROUGH

CANDLE WICK BOBBIN

MELTED WAX PAN

CANDLE ROD

HOPPER

DIE HEAD

CASING OF DUPLEX SCREW EXTRUDER

MOTOR

FIGURE 37

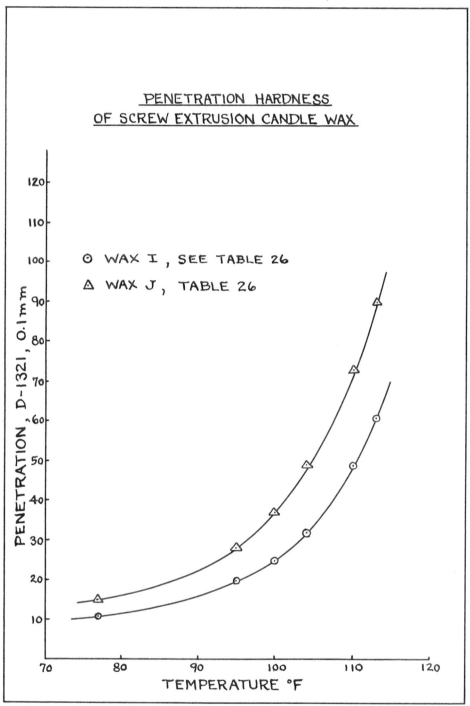

FIGURE 38

Table No. 26

SCREW EXTRUSION CANDLE WAXES

	Wax I	Wax J
Melting Point, D–87, °F.	140.0	140.0
Oil Content, D–721, %	0.3	0.5
Refractive Index at 80°C. (176°F.)	1.4274	1.4294
Penetration Hardness,		
D-1321, 0.1 mm		
at 77°F.	11	15
95°	20	28
100°	25	37
104°	32	49
110°	49	73
113°	61	90
Hydrocarbon Type, by Mol. Sieve[1]		
% Normal Paraffins	90	71
% Non-normals	10	29
Mass Spectra Analysis		
Normal Paraffins, % & C. No.	89.2 (C21–35)	71.3 (C19–38)
Iso-paraffins, % & C. No.	8.3 (C24–36)	16.7 (C26–41)
Cyclo-paraffins, % & C. No.	2.5 (C26–35)	8.2 (C23–38)
Alkyl-benzene, %	—	3.8

[1] Molecular Sieve Analysis

Candle Production by Ram Type Extrusion

In a ram-type extruder there is a reciprocating piston that compresses the wax in a cylinder to extrude a continuous candle rod through an exit die. A typical ram-type extruder is shown in sketch Figure 39.

Wax received as cakes is chipped in a chopper then fed by gravity into the loading chamber of the extruder. Hydraulic pressure supplied to the piston forces the wax chips through several reduction chambers, thereby compressing the chips into one continuous rod.

A typical ram-type extruder operates at a hydraulic pressure of 2,000 psi, which requires a 50-horsepower electric motor. Pressure is supplied to a 14-inch-diameter piston with a 6-inch stroke, six strokes per minute. Wicking is fed through a tube in the last section of the compression chamber, just ahead of the exit die. The wick is embedded within and pulled through by the extruded candle rod. Upon extrusion the candle rod is cut into desired lengths and tipped to expose the wick at one end. To control the

SCHEMATIC OF HYDRAULIC-RAM EXTRUSION OF CANDLES

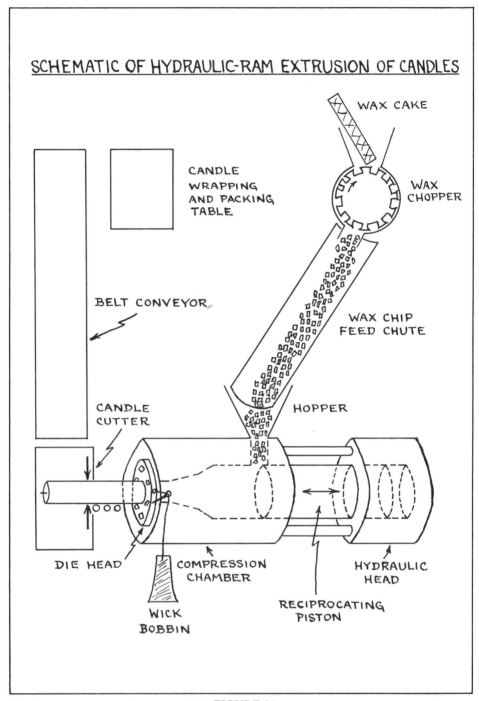

FIGURE 39

wax temperature within the several sections of the cylinder it is jacketed to pass water of controlled temperature through it. With a typical extrusion grade paraffin wax, having a melting point of 130° F., operating temperature within the cylinder is reported to be approximately 75° F. Auxiliary heat may be supplied during start up, with cooling supplied principally during hot weather. Under normal atmospheric temperatures, a temperature satisfactory for compressing the wax into a continuous rod is obtained by normal heat of compression.

A rotary chopper may be employed to chip the wax for feed to the ram-type extruder. Wax slabs are generally fed to a chopper which is driven by a 5-horsepower electric motor. Chips averaging $3/4$ to $1\frac{1}{2}$ inch in longest dimension are produced with the chopper operating at 60 revolutions per minute.

For a wax to perform satisfactorily in this process it must have the following characteristics:

1. It must be brittle enough to chip at normal room temperatures. Chilling the wax if necessary is costly.
2. The chipped wax must be sufficiently non-tacky to allow smooth feed to the hopper and into the compression chamber without clogging.
3. Wax chips must be of such size and handled in such a way as to exclude air from the compressed candle.
4. For smooth extrusion, the wax must be firm as it emerges from the die.
5. Extruded candles should retain dimensional stability. For this reason there should be less than a 5 percent gain in diameter due to expansion of occluded air when the candle is aged in warm air.
6. Candles should be firm enough and hard enough so that they do not block or stick together when wrapped together in one package.
7. The candle wax must burn well and be firm enough to avoid sagging when burned.
8. There should be no sudden expansion of the candle when it is burned. Expansion would be caused by an excess of occluded air within the candle, which expands when the candle is warmed by the flame.

Physical properties of two waxes reported to perform well in a ram-type extruder are shown in Table No. 27. Change in hardness with temperature for the two waxes, Wax K and Wax L, is

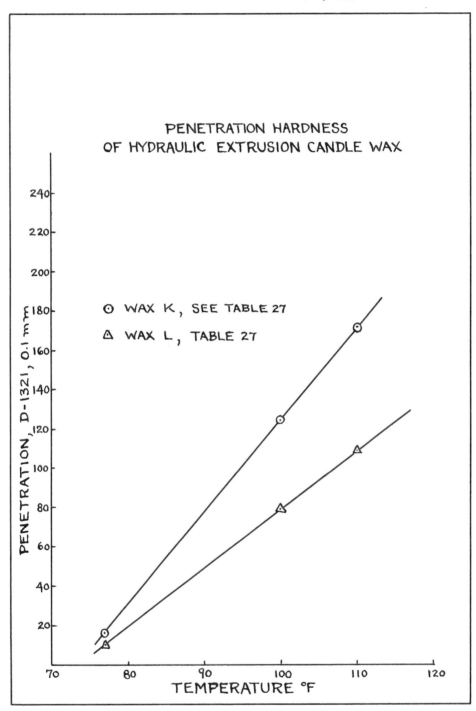

FIGURE 40

presented in Figure 40. A wax with hardness values within the limits of these two waxes would be expected to give excellent performance in a ram-type extruder.

Candle Production by Rotary Drum Extruder

Preparation of wax feed for a rotary drum extruder is similar to that employed in a Weber and Seeländer screw extruder. Wax picked up on the surface of a drum rotating in a wax bath is removed by a knife blade as feed for the extruder. However, in a drum extruder the wax scraped from the drum is mechanically arranged to feed directly into the extruder head. Continued rotation of the drum maintains pressure on the wax being compressed into the extruder head. A drum type extruder is produced in the

Table No. 27

RAM EXTRUSION CANDLE WAXES

	Wax K	Wax L
Melting Point, D–87, °F.	130.0	131.5
Oil Content, D–721, %	0.8	0.2
Refractive Index at 80°C. (176°F.)	1.4276	1.4277
Penetration Hardness, D-1321, 0.1 mm		
at 77°F.	16	10
100°	121	81
110°	172	109
Hydrocarbon Type, by Mol. Sieve[2]		
% Normal Paraffins	83	79
% Non-normals	17	21
Mass Spectra Analysis		
Normal Paraffins, % & C. No.	84.5 (C20–34)	83.9 (C20–33)
Iso-paraffins, % & C. No.	10.4 (C24–36)	12.0 (C25–36)
Cyclo-paraffins, % & C. No.	5.1 (C23–35)	4.1 (C22–34)

[2] Molecular Sieve Analysis

United States by the R. C. Stone Company. A diagrammatic sketch of the equipment is shown in Figure 41.

The R. C. Stone extruder includes a water-cooled drum that rotates on a horizontal axis in a pan of melted wax followed by an extruder head. Level of wax in the pan is held constant by two float valves, one in a wax reservoir, which feeds the pan with melted wax, the other in the wax pan itself. Temperature of melted wax

SCHEMATIC OF ROTARY DRUM EXTRUDER

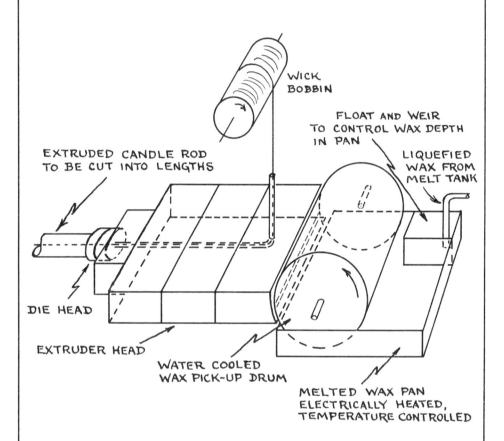

WICK BOBBIN

FLOAT AND WEIR TO CONTROL WAX DEPTH IN PAN

EXTRUDED CANDLE ROD TO BE CUT INTO LENGTHS

LIQUEFIED WAX FROM MELT TANK

DIE HEAD

EXTRUDER HEAD

WATER COOLED WAX PICK-UP DRUM

MELTED WAX PAN ELECTRICALLY HEATED, TEMPERATURE CONTROLLED

NOTES: CONTROLS INCLUDE –

WAX TEMPERATURE AND DEPTH IN PAN.

TEMPERATURE AND RATE OF ROTATION OF DRUM.

TEMPERATURE CONTROL OF EXTRUDER HEAD.

EXTRUSION SECTION–

HEAD BLOCKS BOLTED TOGETHER FOR ACCESSIBILITY.

DIE HEAD READILY REMOVED AND CHANGED.

FIGURE 41

feed is thermostatically controlled in the feed tank and in the wax pan. Drum temperature is controlled by flow rate and temperature of water fed through the drum.

As the drum rotates it picks up and solidifies a layer of wax on its surface. This layer of solidified wax is then scraped from the drum by a doctor blade on a line about 270 angular degrees from the wax pick up line. Thickness and temperature of the wax deposited on the drum are critical for compressing the wax into the extruder head. Wax thickness and temperature are controlled by drum temperature, wax bath temperature, drum depth in melted wax, and speed at which the drum is rotated. All four variables must be carefully controlled for best operation of the extruder. Rotation of the drum hydraulically compacts the wax scraped from the drum into a shielded slit entrance in the extrusion head. Thus, compaction of wax into the extrusion head relates back to thickness, temperature control, and nature of the wax solidified on the drum. Thickness of wax ribbon fed into the extrusion head is controlled by doctor blade adjustment. All conditions should be adjusted to remove a film of adequate thickness and leave a film of wax remaining on the drum. To compress the wax into the extrusion head, as it is being "doctored" from the drum, it is essential that the wax have adequate adherence to the drum surface. This indicates that it must have adequate cohesion and adhesion characteristics at plastic state temperature. Surface temperature of the drum should be above the dew point of the atmosphere to prevent moisture condensation and thus obtain good bonding of wax to the drum. With a good performing wax, pan temperature should be maintained 10 to 20° F. above the melting point of the wax. Cooling water fed to the drum should be 45 to 65° F. and circulated at a rate of about 80 gallons per minute. To control production rate the drum is rotated at speeds up to 10 revolutions per minute, with submergence in melted wax held to a depth of about one-half inch.

It is apparent that the wax should be in a semi-plastic state when it is forced through the compression head. Thus, head temperature should be controlled to maintain the wax within adequate plastic limits. As described for the other extruders, wicking from a bobbin is introduced through a tube with the outlet centered just ahead of the die. In this way the wick is pulled through by the candle rod as it is being extruded.

Physical properties of a wax reported to perform well in the

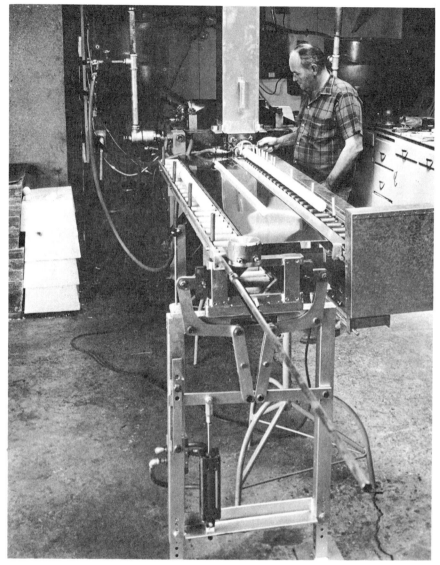

Candle rod extrusion (Courtesy R. C. Stone Co., Alhambra, Cal.)

drum-type extruder are given in Table No. 28. Change in hardness with temperature for this wax is presented in Figure 42. With this wax in the drum extruder, a production rate of approximately 150 pounds per hour is achieved under the following conditions:

Candle Production Conditions
With Wax M in a Rotary Drum Extruder

Wax temperature in storage tank	173°F.
Wax temperature in pan	163°F.
Drum cooling water temperature	66°F.
Drum rate of rotation	4 RPM
Wax thickness on drum	30 mils
Die nose temperature	120°F.

Table No. 28

ROTARY DRUM EXTRUSION CANDLE WAX

	Wax M
Melting Point, D–87, °F.	152.0
Oil Content, D–721, %	0.2
Refractive Index at 80°C.	1.4372
Penetration Hardness, D–1321, 0.1 mm	
at 77°F.	16
100°	35
110°	52
Hydrocarbon Type, by Mol. Sieve[3]	
% Normal Paraffins	55
% Non-normals	45

---

[3] Molecular Sieve Analysis

Water cooled wax pick-up drum on R. C. Stone extruder (Courtesy R. C. Stone Co., Alhambra, Cal.)

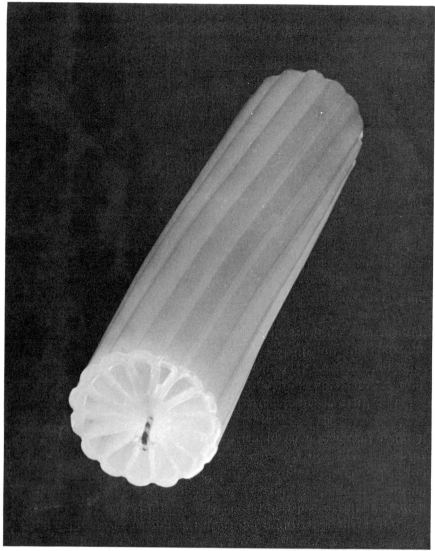

Extruded candle (Courtesy Atlantic Richfield Co., Phila., Pa.)

Summary on Quality Control of Extruded Candles

Production of satisfactory candles by extrusion is to a large extent dependent upon characteristics of the paraffin wax employed. With some waxes, extrusion head temperature control may be critical and require temperature control within a narrow range.

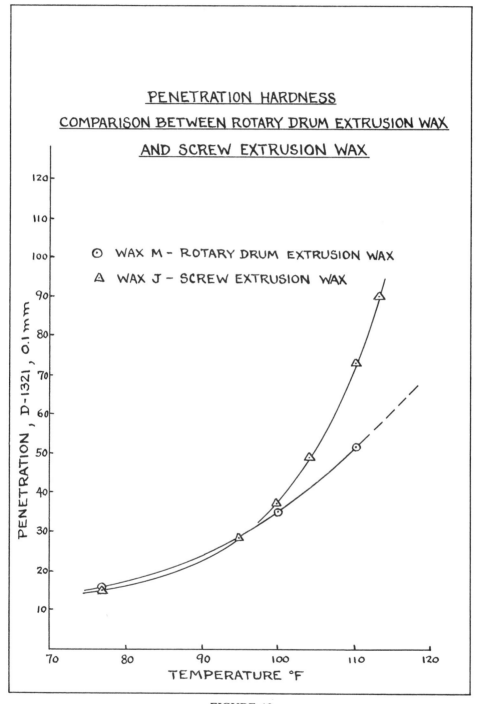

FIGURE 42

The preferred wax would perform well over a relatively broad solid state temperature range. Indications are that the wax should be controlled to a temperature within the plastic state, which occurs 20 to 30° F. below its melting point and at a temperature above its crystalline state. With the wax in the plastic state it is more uniformly compressed and extruded than in the crystalline state.

Temperature range within which the plastic state of a paraffin wax exists depends upon melting point distribution and iso-paraffin content. Breadth of cut and iso-paraffin content of a wax may be indirectly indicated by an extended cooling curve on the wax by the ASTM D–87 test method. An increase in melting point distribution and an increase in iso-paraffin content of the petroleum wax shortens the melting point flat and makes the transition temperature less distinct. In a very broad spectrum wax with an iso-paraffin content above about 50 percent there usually are no distinct melting point or transition temperature flats. A wax with a long melting point and transition temperature flat would be hard at room temperature and have a very critical plastic temperature range. These two types of paraffin wax would perform poorly in extrusion. The second would be too hard and brittle, the first too soft and plastic, perhaps even sticky. Indications are that for best extrusion performance the wax should be moderately broad cut and have an iso-paraffin content of about 30 percent. This is inferred from a short melting point flat followed by an indistinct transition temperature.

A direct measure of wax suitability for extrusion would be by determining the rate at which it softens with increase in temperature. This may be determined by measuring penetration hardness by the ASTM D–1321 test method with increase in temperature. The unsatisfactory, close-cut, highly normal paraffin wax exhibits a sharp increase in penetration values with increase in temperature. A satisfactory broad-cut wax with a moderate iso-paraffin wax content shows a gradual softening with increase in temperature. For examples see Figures 38, 40, and 42.

Indications are that an extended cooling curve and penetration hardness with change in temperature may be jointly employed to evaluate the suitability of a paraffin wax for production of candles by extrusion. It also appears that these two criteria may be used to set the best operating temperatures for the wax being used.

Criticality of extruder head temperature is best determined experimentally with each type of equipment and wax. The best operating temperature range for a given wax may then be related to penetration hardness of the wax over that temperature range. Possible suitability of and operating temperature for any other wax may then be inferred from penetration hardness values of the wax with change in temperature. The transition temperature range in an extended cooling curve may also be used to determine the suitability of a wax relative to a known satisfactory wax.

For an extruded candle to have a uniform surface appearance it is important that the entire body of wax in the extruder be maintained at a uniform temperature. Air occluded in the extruded candle wax, which tends to expand the candle on aging and burning, may also be traceable to inadequate or non-uniform temperature control of the wax in the extruder.

In seeking a quotation on the cost of a given type of candle extruder, the following specification variables should be considered.

1. Ease of changing extruder die.
2. Size and shape limitations of the die.
3. Maximum rate of production.
4. Temperature controls required on feed and extruder.
5. Space required for the unit and auxiliary equipment.
6. Auxiliary equipment, tankage, and temperature controls required.
7. Candle finishing equipment needed, including cutting, trimming, and wrapping equipment.

11
Unique and Novel Candles

A book on candles would not be complete without a discussion on unique and novel candles. The home candle maker may make these candles for use as gifts or for display as conversation pieces. The possible varieties of candles are almost endless. As previously stated, candle variety is limited only by the imagination, with originality being paramount. Of the several basic techniques previously described, any one or a combination of these techniques may be used to produce the completely unique candle. Considerable pleasure may be derived in making a one-of-a-kind useful object. This is most certainly true in making a unique candle. Pleasure may be further amplified if during a conversation on candles the inventive way for making the unique candle is described.

With there being so many possible varieties of unique candles, a list can do little more than give ideas. It is with this in mind that the following list is presented, with a brief discussion to suggest production procedure.

Wax Chip Candles

Wax chip candles make a unique gift wherein the pleasure of making a candle is shared with the receiver of the gift. A fancy jar or a hob-nail-type glass of suitable size is suggested for use as a container for the candle. Colored wax chips are made by casting a quantity of dyed wax in a pan then breaking the solidified wax into irregular shaped pieces. This may be done by removing the wax cake from the pan then striking it with a blunt metal bar or by driving a cold chisel into it at odd angles. A prewaxed

WAX CHIP CANDLE

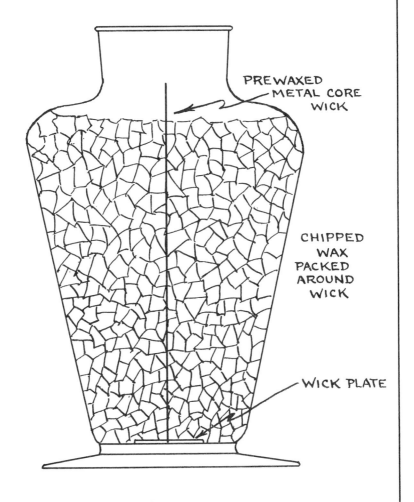

PREWAXED
METAL CORE
WICK

CHIPPED
WAX
PACKED
AROUND
WICK

WICK PLATE

ANY PLAIN OR FANCY GLASS JAR MAY BE USED

FIGURE 43

metal-core wick with a wick tin fastened at one end is supplied separately. The wick length should be about ½ inch more than the depth of the jar or glass supplied. Colored wax chips are packaged separately from the wick and jar, along with instructions on making the finished candle. To make the finished candle the wick is placed straight and centered into the jar bottom with the tin flat. Wax chips are then filled into the jar, and the candle is thus ready to be burned.

A brittle, close-cut wax with a 130 to 140° F. melting point should be used to avoid having the wax chips stick together in the package. Wax D or Wax E, previously described, are suggested for this use. A 34–40 metal-core wick is suggested with this wax and a jar of up to two inches in diameter. If a larger diameter jar or higher melting point wax is used, a larger size metal-core wick should be employed. A sketch of this type candle is given in Figure 43.

Driftwood Candles

Salt-water-soaked and weathered driftwood is ideally suited for use in providing an artistic embellishment to a molded candle. The driftwood may be so shaped to hold a candle or it may be casted into the side of a candle to act as a background. The natural form of the wood should be preserved and taken advantage of in designing the candle. It may be flattened on one end or on a side to act as the base upon which it can stand. Hollowed out sections can be used as containers into which candles with metal-core wicks may be casted. Large hollows taking several pounds of wax would be provided with several wicks to make a multi-wicked candle.

A beachcomber candle may be made by using damp beach sand packed and shaped into a mold in which a piece of driftwood is included for an artistic effect. With the mold shaped, the wood is positioned in the mold to become a background for the candle. Metal-core wicks are placed into mold, whereupon melted wax is poured into it and allowed to solidify. Moisture evaporates from the sand while the wax is solidifying. To retain its shape, the sand mold should be kept moist until the candle has completely solidified. Dried residual sand may be brushed from the finished candle. This type of candle is shown in Figure 44.

DRIFTWOOD CANDLE

HOLLOWED DRIFTWOOD

SAND MOLD,
DRIFTWOOD
INSERT AS
PART OF
CANDLE

WET SAND
HOLLOWED
AS MOLD

METAL CORE
WICK TO BE
CENTERED
IN MOLD

FIGURE 44

Rolled Candles

Candles may be made by wrapping a sheet of plastic wax as a helix around a prewaxed wick, layer upon layer, to build up a rolled candle of desired diameter. Either a sheet of plastic wax, or wax warmed enough to be in the plastic state, may be employed. To cast the wax into a sheet, melted wax may be poured onto suitable wax-release non-fibrous paper or cloth, for example Syloff treated paper (see Figure 45). When solidified the sheet of wax is trimmed and removed from the paper for use in wrapping around the wick. To smooth surface irregularities and remove the side ridge, the candle is passed through a heated die.

Shell Candle

A shell candle, having a carved surface appearance, may be made by casting a ¼- to ⅜-inch thickness of plastic wax in a flat bed of carved plaster or dense non-porous wood. The surface of the flat mold is carved to have a pleasing and interesting design. The surface area of the mold is made to have one dimension equal to the height of the candle, with the other dimension ½ inch longer than the desired circumference of the finished candle. The wax casting picks up the design of the carved surface.

In carving the mold surface a flat and level retainer wall of uniform thickness is left remaining around the perimeter of the mold. Mold depth is cut to provide a ¼- to ⅜-inch thickness to solidified molded wax. Before casting the wax, the mold is sprayed with a silicone mold release agent. Melted wax is then poured into the mold and allowed to solidify. When completely solidified the wax is carefully removed from the mold and formed into a candle shell on a cylindrical mandrel with the carved impression on the outside. The mandrel should be of such a diameter as to allow the two ends of the casted wax to be overlapped. The overlapped ends are then sealed using a low temperature soldering iron with a broad flat tip, or by use of a suitable sealing iron. The cylindrical shell is then slid off of the mandrel, whereupon the shell is supplied with a wick and filled with wax.

To fill the shell with wax it is stood firmly on a flat surface and temporarily sealed around the outside at the base with a soft modeling clay. A prewaxed metal-core wick, with wick plate at the bottom

MAKING A ROLLED CANDLE

STEP ONE

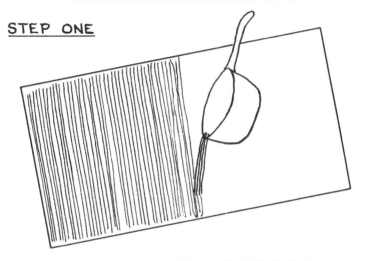

CAST THIN FILM OF WAX ON MOLD RELEASE
COATED PAPER OR CLOTH.

STEP TWO

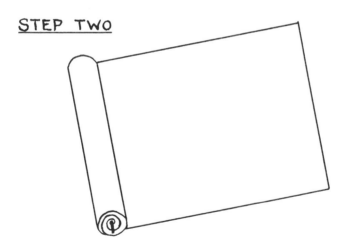

WAX FILM ROLLED AROUND PREWAXED
SQUARE BRAIDED WICK.

FIGURE 45

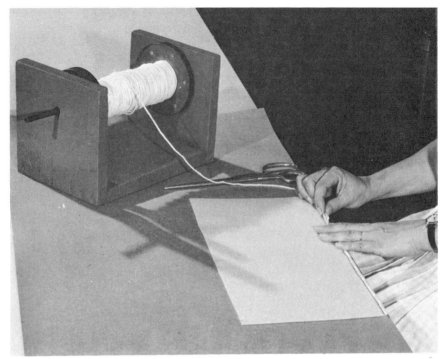

Start of rolling a candle (Courtesy A. I. Root Candle Co., Medina, Ohio)

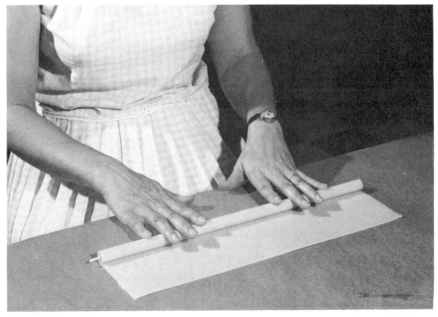

Rolling a candle (Courtesy A. I. Root Candle Co., Medina, Ohio)

Smoothing a rolled candle by passing through a heated die (Courtesy A. I. Root Candle Co., Medina, Ohio)

end, is centered in the shell. A foamed wax, or low-melting wax, is then used to fill the candle shell. If a high-melting-point wax, for example 170° F. M.P., is used for the shell and a low-melting-point wax is used as fill, the shell will act as a mantle when the candle is burned and will not be consumed. A 125° F. melting point wax is suggested for fill, for example Wax B previously described. It may be foamed by beating air into it at a temperature slightly below its melting point. By use of foamed wax the fill will be consumed in a shorter period of time than with a solid fill of wax of equal volume when it is burned. This helps to preserve the shell for reuse. With the shell filled with wax, the clay dam is removed from the base to release the finished candle. The steps taken to make a shell candle are shown in Figure 46.

Holiday Season Molded Candles

A great variety of holiday and special season molded candles may be made (see Chapter 9 on molded candles). For example pilsner glasses may be used to mold a Christmas-tree-shaped candle, which may then be decorated with foamed wax sprinkled with

MAKING A SHELL CANDLE

STEP ONE

CARVED WOOD
OR PLASTER MOLD

FILL MOLD WITH MELTED HIGH MELT
WAX AND ALLOW TO SOLIDIFY.

STEP TWO

WOOD MANDREL

OVERLAP
SEALED
WITH
HEATED
ROD

OVERLAP HEAT SEAL MOLDED
CANDLE SHELL ON MANDREL.

STEP THREE

METAL
CORE
WICK

RUBBER
MAT

CANDLE SHELL FILLED
AROUND WICK WITH
FOAMED LOW MELT WAX.

FIGURE 46

glitter. Easter egg candles may be made using plaster or flexible rubber molds as described in the Appendix. The egg-shaped candle should be casted with a flat on the broad end so that the candle can stand in a vertical position with the narrow end up.

Seasonal garlands and decorations may also be devised to decorate and display candles for special occasions.

As has been described in the several chapters on candle production there are many types of candles that may be made. There are also many degrees of interest in making candles. These range from a home hobby, through a home business, to the ultimate of automated commercial candle production. Many commercial candle manufacturers have started small and with originality have grown to a large profitable business.

12
Establishing a Candle Business

Candle making has recently become a growth industry. More small candle shops are being established with each passing year. Most start small then grow with the expanding market. Candle shops start in many ways. Some start by selling candles made by major manufacturers, others start as an outgrowth of making candles as a hobby. Shops that grow from a hobby make some of their candles and fill in their line with a variety of purchased candles. Very often the small shop will expand into making the candles that sales experience indicates sell best.

Most candle shops find it practical and profitable to carry a line of candle accessories. These include candle holders, candle rings, and garlands. Many types of candle holders may be made available to the candle shop customer. Candle holders may be made of a variety of materials and in a variety of shapes and forms. They would include single candle holders, sometimes known as candlesticks, as well as elaborate sconces and candelabras. These may be made of pewter, brass, silver, ornamental iron, glass, china, or wood.

The candle retail shop may be a speciality shop carrying only candles and candle accessories. Experience has shown that candle speciality shops do well in resort towns and at historical sites. However, in urban and suburban areas, candles are very often carried as a department in a gift and greeting card shop. Greeting card companies and chinaware companies now have candle making subsidiaries that supply gift and card shops.

With candles representing an ever-growing appreciation for a slower more gracious living in a more affluent society, sales of candles have doubled in the last ten years. The "kitchen hobby"

Specialty candle shop (Courtesy Candle Creations, Reading, Pa.)

candle maker who has grown with this market to establish a retail candle shop is faced with the choice to expand production equipment and facilities, or to purchase candles at wholesale. In many instances there is a transition period during which the candle shop business is more profitably built up by selling candles bought at wholesale. During this period production facilities are judiciously expanded in keeping with an economic balance.

In expanding candle production facilities from a profitable hobby to a candle business there comes a time to shift from handling wax in slabs to handling wax in bulk liquid storage, in order to economically further expand production. With still further expansion in production, the candle shop may then serve not only as a retail store but also as a show room for establishing and expanding a wholesale business. Several major candle manufacturing companies have followed this route. Others with the desire and business ability will do likewise.

The transition from use of paraffin wax as 10-pound slabs—60 pounds per carton or 1000 pounds per skid—to use of liquid wax held in bulk storage is a major step. Liquid wax in 10,000- to

Candle creations (Courtesy Candle Creations, Reading, Pa.)

20,000-pound lots is delivered to the candle plant by the refiner in insulated tank trucks and railroad tank cars. Tankage, transfer lines, and heating facilities are installed at the candle plant to accommodate the bulk handling of wax. If more than one grade of wax is used, a separate tank for each must be installed. If waxes are blended or additives are employed to provide a special candle wax for use, a blending tank or proportionating equipment is also needed. Capital expenditure for this equipment is written off by reduced unit cost for the wax. Economies in production lead toward improved profitability and expanded sales. The ultimate in efficiency would be to completely automate candle production, for example by installation of candle extruders.

To receive and handle wax in bulk, transfer lines and storage tanks must be heated and insulated. Steam generating equipment, with steam coils in the tanks and steam tracer coils on transfer lines, are generally used. Steam lines with couplings are also used to attach to coils in tank trucks and tank cars to melt the wax that may have solidified while being transported, so that the truck or car may be unloaded. Thermostatic controls should be used on the tanks to prevent the wax in storage from being overheated. Thermostatically controlled electrical strip heaters are generally used to regulate temperature in automated candle making equipment.

Care should always be taken to handle wax in a safe manner. Remember, overheated wax in the presence of air will burn. In addition to safety reasons, overheating the wax should be avoided to prevent odor and color degradation of the wax. Spills should be avoided, but if they occur they should be promptly cleaned up. Local fire and safety codes must be carefully followed. Conversely, solid wax presents relatively little safety hazard, as for example when chipped as feed for a ram-type candle extruder. In this case the wax would be used as cakes rather than from liquid storage.

Handling of liquid paraffin wax is to be given thought.

1. *It pays to be safe in handling petroleum wax.* As indicated in Chapter 4, petroleum wax has a rather low flash point. The wise candle maker avoids overheating petroleum wax to prevent fires. Depending upon the composition and grade of wax, its auto-ignition temperature may be as low as 400° F. If melted wax is absorbed into porous insulation on heated wax transfer lines, the absorbed wax is gradually "cracked" or degraded by the heat to a lower flash point material. Should this cracked wax be ignited, the temperature of the remaining wax is raised by the flame and the porous insulation acts like a wick in a candle to feed the flame. Fire can then very easily spread over a wide area. Wax spilled in adjoining areas may then further spread the fire. The best reason for good housekeeping and good wax temperature control is to avoid a destructive fire.

Safe practice for the home hobbyist to employ in melting candle wax is by use of a double boiler type of installation. With this procedure water is heated, which in turn heats and melts the wax in the second container. In this way the wax will not be heated higher than the boiling point of the water (i.e., 212° F. at normal atmospheric pressure). Temperature of melted wax should be controlled, not only to prevent fires but also to provide best pouring temperature for candle molding. The home candle maker may use a relatively inexpensive thermometer to check temperatures. Large candle plants do well by employing thermostatic controls in storage tanks and unit supply tanks.

It is wise for large candle plants to have a water-fog or steam-fog system installation as a good way to fight a wax fire. An asbestos sheet may be used by the home candle maker as a cover to extinguish a wax fire. By covering burning wax with the asbestos sheet air is excluded thus killing the fire.

2. *Color and oxidation stability* of wax in liquid storage is a major concern of candle companies that produce white candles. Color darkening of the wax due to oxidation is thus to be avoided. Certain metals, principally copper, zinc, and aluminum, are known to catalyze or stimulate oxidation of melted wax. Accordingly, these metals should not contact liquid wax. Black iron is least active in this regard and is recommended for use. It is also least expensive for use in fabricating melted-wax storage tanks, transfer lines, and candle molding equipment. In all cases rate of oxidation increases with increase in temperature. As a general rule the rate of wax oxidation doubles every 10° C. increase in temperature. For best operation, bulk storage of paraffin wax in the liquid state should be at lowest possible liquid temperature. Where the wax is to be used at a higher temperature than that at which it is stored, a small secondary heating tank may be used to supply the wax to the candle equipment. Either electric strip heaters or steam coils may be installed in the small supply tank to raise the wax to use temperature. In this way, with rapid usage of the wax only a relatively small quantity of it is held at the elevated temperature for a short period of time. Local over-heating of the wax should also be guarded against. Stagnant pockets and corners should be eliminated from the equipment. It is also helpful to arrange for uniform distribution of heating elements in the equipment and to slowly circulate melted wax in tankage during storage. An oxidation inhibitor may be added to the wax to guard against accidental

overheating, as pointed out in Chapter 6 on wax additives.

One last word to those contemplating the candle business: Candle production is a profitable business, with a high rate of return for a minimum capital investment. In comparison to many other businesses, it may be started small and grow with the market. A retail candle shop should be located where the women are, or where they tend to go, for example shopping centers, vacation and historical spots, or near office buildings where a high percentage of women are employed. It is reported as a fact that 95 percent of the candles purchased are sold to women.

Appendix

Plaster Candle Molds

Objects having a simple shape and form may be duplicated as a candle by use of plaster molds made of the objects. Cylindrical and simple three-dimensional art objects lend themselves well to duplication as candles by use of such molds. Plaster, sometimes known as Plaster of Paris, is added to water to make a slurry, which is applied to the model, allowed to dry, and then removed from the model to provide a mold for duplicating the model. If the model is a porous material it must first be coated with a pore sealant to obtain fidelity of reproduction. A parting agent may have to be used on the model to obtain clean release and separation of the dried plaster from the model. To make a mold of a rather intricately shaped model it is usually necessary to make a two-part mold with a natural parting line established between the two halves. Having made the plaster mold, the pores of the plaster molding-surface should be sealed to make it impervious to liquid wax. Details of these operations are discussed and described as follows.

The United States Gypsum Company is a major producer and supplier of plasters found by experience to be most suitable for making candle molds. Several grades of plaster are available. Among them there are differences in setting time, setting expansion, surface hardness, and compression strength when dried. United States Gypsum's Ultracal 30 is suggested as being most satisfactory for use in making candle molds. Ultracal 30, when made to recommended consistency of *35 to 38 parts water* and *100 parts by weight plaster,* produces a slurry that is pourable and has a setting time of 20 to 30 minutes, with a setting expansion of 0.0003 inches per inch. Compression strength of the dried plaster is 7300 pounds per square inch.

The plaster slurry develops strength during set-up time by forming very small interlaced needle-like crystals. To develop maximum strength it is important that the recommended ratio of water to plaster be employed. If for example an excess of water is used, the cured plaster will have lowered strength. Both water and plaster should be weighed to obtain an exact mix. Volumetric measurements lead to errors and should not be used. Dry plaster should always be added to the water by carefully distributing the weighed quantity of plaster into the weighed amount of water. The mix is then allowed to sit undisturbed for 2 to 3 minutes, after which it should be mixed thoroughly until the slurry creams and slightly thickens. Usually 2 to 5 minutes of mixing is sufficient. Small quantities of mix, ranging from 5 to 25 pounds, are usually prepared by hand mixing with a spatula for about 2 minutes. Larger batches of mix, ranging from 25 to 50 pounds, are made best by using an electric drill equipped with a rubber disc on the end of a mixer shaft. Temperature of the water used will influence setting time. Warm water, 130 to 140° F., accelerates setting time. Conversely, cold water, 50 to 60° F., extends fluidity and setting time, without affecting the finished cast. A minor effect is that setting-expansion is somewhat greater when cold water is used. Mixing time also influences setting time. The longer the slurry is mixed the shorter will be the setting time.

Models of certain materials may have to be sealed—and in addition a parting agent applied—before they can be used from which to make a plaster mold. For example, models of wood and plaster must be sealed to avoid moisture absorption from the plaster slurry. Wood grain is swelled and the model distorted by moisture. Fresh plaster may adhere to an untreated plaster model. As would be expected, impervious materials, for example metal, glass, or plastics, do not require sealing. An excellent sealer for wood and plaster is a quick drying lacquer applied by brush or spray gun. Several thin coats are preferred to one thick coat. A parting agent is applied to the model to prevent adhesion of the plaster cast. It should protect and lubricate the surface of the model. To do this effectively it should spread easily and uniformly over the surface of the model as a thin continuous, water insoluble film. *Release or parting agents* that satisfy these requirements include:

1. Stearic acid dissolved in kerosene. Approximately 4 ounces of stearic acid are melted and dissolved in one pint of kerosene. Stir until complete solution is obtained.

2. A petrolatum (petroleum jelly) dissolved in kerosene, two parts of kerosene to one part of petrolatum.

3. Camphor dissolved in alcohol is useful on models having extremely fine details. A 10 percent solution of camphor in alcohol may be used.

The parting agent is applied to the model with a soft bristled brush. If brush marks appear in using either one of the first two agents, the solution should be further diluted with kerosene.

Having applied a sealer and a parting agent to the model as needed, it is now ready to be used to make a plaster mold. Shape and intricacy of the model is to be considered in setting up the mold. Release of the plaster mold from the model is obviously related to the intricacies in shape and form of the model. A two-part mold may have to be made, keeping in mind the lines of the model and that an open end must be provided in the mold to allow filling with wax to make a candle replica. With a tall model, most suitable for use in making candles, a two-part mold with a vertical parting line along a natural edge or mid line is suggested. Best practice is to draw the parting line on the model with an indelible pencil before the parting compound is applied. A half mold is then made by applying fresh plaster to the model up to this line on one side. The plaster should be built to an adequate thickness for mold strength. When fully built up the plaster is allowed to dry and harden, then while still in place the half-mold is carefully trimmed to a sharp, clean parting surface. Alignment holes are cut into the parting surfaces of the half-mold, and the model is then carefully removed. Parting surfaces are sealed with a lacquer or shellac, which when dry, the surfaces are coated with a parting compound. The model is then returned to the half-mold, whereupon plaster is applied to the second half of the model. It is important that the alignment holes in the first half-mold be filled with a continuation of plaster from the second half-mold. When the second part of the mold has dried, the two halves are parted and removed from the model.

The inside surface of both mold halves are then sealed with lacquer or shellac to make the surface impervious against wax absorption. The mold is then ready to be assembled for use. The two halves are fitted together and adhesive tape is applied over the parting lines, whereupon the mold is held together with rubber bands or cord. With the mold assembled, the wick is put in place. Melted wax is then poured into the mold and allowed to solidify to produce a candle replica.

A metal-core wick is suggested for use. Wick size is selected as indicated in the Chapter on Wicking and the discussion on molding a candle with melted wax. If the closed end of the mold is to be the top of the candle, a hole is drilled into the closed end to accommodate the wick. If the open end of the mold is to be the top of the candle, the wick may be placed as in making a seven-day votive light.

With care a plaster mold may be used over and over to make many candle duplicates of the original model.

To duplicate an intricately shaped model as a candle, use of a rubber mold is to be preferred over the use of plaster. A rubber mold has the advantage in that it may be flexed away from the model as well as from the wax candle replica to obtain release. Preparation of a flexible rubber mold is described in the following discussion.

Flexible Rubber Candle Molds

A plaster cast is made first to act as a support for the flexible rubber mold of the model. Depending upon the complexity of the model, the plaster mold may be made in one or more pieces. Space is provided between the model and the plaster support by covering the model with paper-mache (paper soaked in water). This may be accomplished by using paper pulped to a slurry in water, or by criss-crossing water-soaked strips of paper on the model. The thickness of paper applied to the model determines the thickness of the flexible rubber mold when it is made. Contours of the model are followed in applying the paper, and they are built to a suggested thickness of about 0.25 inch.

When the model has been covered with wet paper, the paper is allowed to dry, whereupon the covered model is suspended in the center of a box. The box should be of such a size to allow reasonable space on all sides of the model to be filled with plaster. With most models the base is the largest flat area, and it should be supported upper most in the box. It is thus arranged to provide an opening in the rubber mold, which allows filling it with wax to make the candle replica.

With the model suspended in the box, plaster is poured into the box to cover all but the upper most base of the model. Plaster should be added to the box until it is level with the base of the model. When the plaster has hardened, the mold is carefully removed from the box and the model is removed from the mold. If the shape and form of the model restricts easy removal from the mold, it is cut into two sections along natural parting lines. This may be accomplished with a small diameter thin circular saw, being careful to cut through just to the paper layer and thus avoid marring the model.

Having the model out of the mold, the paper layers are removed and all paper bits and fibers cleaned from the surface. The plaster mold surface is then sealed with several thin coats of shellac, whereupon both the model and the plaster mold cavity are sprayed with a neutral soap solution or silicone mold release.

The model is then suspended evenly spaced within the mold cavity. The space between the mold and model is to be filled with liquid rubber to form the flexible mold. Either D.P.R. depolymerized isoprene or C.M.C. polysulfide polymer, both supplied by the Perma-Flex Company, may be used. The rubber compound is mixed as directed by accompanying instructions. The prepared rubber is then poured into the space between the mold and the model, being careful not to leave any air holes. At ordinary room temperatures, about 20 hours are allowed for the rubber to cure. When the rubber has cured, the plaster mold is removed; then the rubber mold is carefully flexed from the model. If difficulty is encountered, a jet of compressed air is helpful in stripping the rubber mold from the model after parting at the open edge has been started.

To prepare for casting a candle copy of the model, the rubber mold is reassembled into the cavity of the plaster mold, which acts as a rigid backup for the flexible mold. Care should be taken to align the surfaces of the two with each other. With the open end of the assembled mold up, a rigid metal wire of suitable size and length is positioned in the mold around which wax is poured to provide a wick hole when the wax has solidified and the wire withdrawn. The wire is positioned in the mold cavity in the same way as the wick in the finished candle, to control burning of the candle. Diameter of the wire used should be slightly larger than the diameter of the wick chosen for use in the candle.

Melted wax is poured into the assembled mold and allowed to cool. When thoroughly solidified the mold is disassembled, and the wire is pulled from the molded wax and replaced with a metal-core wick. The wick should be crimped into a wick tin at the lower end so that the tin may be forced into the base of the candle to hold it in place.

Use of a flexible rubber mold allows high fidelity reproduction of intricately shaped models as a smooth surfaced, good appearing candle. By use of a wax with a melting point of about 150° F. and containing 1 percent of Elvax 210, a candle with a fine-grain structure and good strength characteristics is obtained. Wick size is chosen to match the melting point of the wax, size and shape of the candle and to provide the burning performance required. An undersized wick is used to provide a flame that will burn down into the candle replica, rather than destroy or consume the candle.

Candle Wicking Detailed

The major supplier of candle wicking in the United States is the Atkins and Pearce Company, Pearl and Pike Streets, Cincinnati, Ohio 45202.

Three types of wicking are produced for candle use namely metal-core wick, flat-plaited wick, and square-braided wick. Each type is made in several diameters identified in the trade by a code number.

METAL-CORE WICK

Metal-core wick is made with a lead wire core surrounded by a woven cotton sleeve. The cotton fibers in the sleeve wick melted wax up into the flame where the wax is vaporized to be burned. In burning a candle containing this wick, the lead core melts into beads in the hot part of the flame which then drop off to effectively shorten the wick above the surface of melted wax, and thereby control flame height. Flame size and burning rate are controlled by wick diameter.

Identification and use of metal-core wick is as follows:

Table 1-A

Code Identification	Common Usage
44–32–18	Large Diameter Candle of High Melt Wax
44–24–18	Large Diameter Candle of Moderate Melt Wax
44–20–18	Moderate Diameter Candle of Moderate Melt Wax
36–24–24	Moderate Diameter Candle of Low Melt Wax
34–40	Jar Candles made of Very Low Melt Wax
32–24	Small Jar Candles of Very Low Melt Wax

With a metal core, the wick is used where it is to be self-supporting and have a degree of rigidity.

FLAT-PLAITED WICK

Plaited and braided cotton wicking are used in rigid candles that are self-supporting, in which only a small pool of melted wax is to form at the base of the flame when the candle is burned.

A plaited wick curls into a hook in the flame when the candle is burned. The tip of the hook extends to the hot outer part of the flame, where it is consumed to effectively shorten the wick above the surface of melted wax and thereby control flame height.

Wick size should be increased with increase in melting point of the wax used, and with an increase in diameter of the candle. Presence of high-melting-point additives in the candle wax, for example polyethylene, ethylene vinyl-acetate copolymer, or a high melting microwax, require use of a larger wick than would normally be used with a given-melting-point wax.

Identification and use of flat-plaited wick is as follows:

Table 1-B

Identification	Typical Candle Use
42 Ply	4-inch diameter candle, 150° M.P. Wax
36 Ply	3½-inch diameter candle, 150° M.P. Wax
30 Ply	3-inch diameter candle, 140° M.P. Wax
24 Ply	2-inch diameter candle, 135° M.P. Wax
15 Ply	1-inch diameter candle, 130° M.P. Wax

SQUARE-BRAIDED WICK

The curl that forms in a plaited wick tends to put the flame off center in the candle when burned. A square-braided wick stands rather straight when burned, which keeps the flame centered in the candle. The tip of this wick is consumed in the hot upper part of the flame, thereby controlling flame height.

Trade designation and use of square-braided wick is as follows:

Table 1-C

Designation	Typical Candle Use
#5	5-inch diameter candle, 160° M.P. Wax
#3	4-inch diameter candle, 150° M.P. Wax
#1	3½-inch diameter candle, 150° M.P. Wax
2/0	3-inch diameter candle, 140° M.P. Wax
5/0	2-inch diameter candle, 135° M.P. Wax
6/0	2-inch diameter candle, 130° M.P. Wax
6/0TT	1-inch diameter candle, 130° M.P. Wax

Burning Evaluation of Candles

A well-balanced candle will burn evenly with a smokeless flame without production of excess melted wax to drip or gutter from the candle. The larger the flame size, the greater is the tendency for the flame to smoke and produce soot. Also, with increase in flame size, the greater is the rate of heat production melting wax in excess of that required to support the flame. Excess melted wax tends to drip or gutter from the candle. Flame size is controlled primarily by wick size and to some extent by melting point of the wax used in making the candle.

It is suggested that prototypes of candles to be produced for sale be evaluated under standardized burning conditions. For reproducible evaluations, a temperature-controlled, draft-free room should be used. To reduce drafts, candles may be burned within a fine mesh wire-screen enclosure.

EVALUATION OF DIPPED AND MOLDED TAPERS

Dipped and molded tapers, including dinner candles and tavern candles, burn best when there is essentially no excess melted wax beyond that required to feed the flame. Under this condition the candle is said to burn with a dry socket. Candles should be evaluated under typical conditions of use. In some instances, as with tavern candles that are burned in a spring loaded cylinder, the candle is required to burn a given number of hours. To evaluate this type of candle it is placed into a representative cylinder, pressed down against the spring in the bottom of the cylinder, and then the cap through which the wick extends is inserted onto the top of the cylinder to hold the candle in place. The cap and cylinder, being metal, conduct heat away from the base of the flame and tend to keep the candle socket dry.

In evaluating the burning quality of a candle, it is weighed before being burned and again after burning is completed and the flame extinguished. Burning rate is calculated from the burning time and weight of candle burned during that time. Calculate and record the average weight of candle burned during one hour. Wax that may have dripped or guttered from the candle is collected and weighed. Weight of dripped wax is calculated as a percent of the wax burned. The character, height, and tendency of the flame to soot is observed and recorded. To pinpoint desired candle performance direct comparisons are to be made among several candles. Several wick sizes and melting-point waxes in a given type and diameter of candle may be related in making the comparisons.

EVALUATION OF CANDLES CONTAINED IN JARS

Candles contained in jars should burn without production of soot and without remaining unburned wax on the jar wall. In addition, some jar candles are required to burn a given length of time, for example the seven-day votive light. As with tapers, burning rate is determined and flame character noted. In addition the amount of unburned wax remaining on the jar wall, known as hang-up, is determined as a percent of the wax burned; soot deposited on the jar wall is rated arbitrarily on a relative scale.

Hang-up is reduced by using a lower-melting-point wax or a wax containing less high-melting components. If a larger wick is used for a greater rate of heat production to thereby reduce hang-up, burning time for the quantity of wax contained in the jar may be excessively shortened. In addition, soot may be produced if the flame is too large, along with the higher burning rate. Again as with tapers, the correct wick size and melting-point wax for desired performance is to be determined in comparative evaluations.

EVALUATION OF LARGE DIAMETER CANDLES

Large diameter candles (that is candles above two inches in diameter) include those that are to form peripheral petals of wax when the candle is burned. Petal-forming candles, sometimes known as foliating or angel-winged candles, are usually burned intermittently for about three hours each time. It is therefore suggested that these candles be evaluated as they are used.

Burning rate, amount of guttered wax, and degree of foliation are the three observations made on large diameter foliating-type candles. Burning rate and amount of guttered wax is measured quantitatively by weight as described for tapers. Degree of foliation is evaluated arbitrarily on a relative scale.

Correct wick size and wax for desired performance may be determined in comparative evaluations. Foliation is related to wall thickness of unburned wax and to the plasticity of the wall of wax at flame temperature. These are dependent upon the diameter of the candle, the size of wick employed, and the characteristics of the wax, including melting point and iso-paraffin content. Wall thickness is best reduced by using a slightly lower melting point wax or by decreasing the diameter of the candle. An increase in wick size to produce more heat and melt more wax may tend to produce soot and a higher burning rate than desired, and is not

Candle burning evaluation (Courtesy Atlantic Richfield Co., Phila., Pa.)

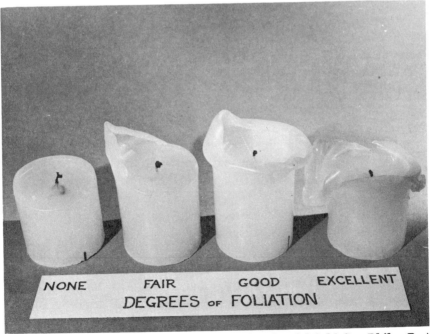

Qualitative candle foliation (Courtesy Atlantic Richfield Co., Phila., Pa.)

recommended. A complete discussion on foliating candles is given in the chapter on molded candles.

Glossary of Common Terms and Standard Test Methods

ALCOHOL—A carbon-hydrogen compound characterized by a hydroxyl group, i.e., –OH, in the molecule.

ANTI-OXIDANT—A chemical added to a substance in small amounts to prevent degradation of the substance by oxygen.

BLOCKING TEMPERATURE—The minimum temperature at which two wax surfaces will stick together when in intimate contact.

CATALYST—A material that stimulates a reaction. For example, copper stimulates the oxidation of melted paraffin wax.

CONGEALING TEMPERATURE—That temperature at which a melted substance solidifies when cooled; it may be measured by A.S.T.M. method D-938.

CONTRACTION—Noted as coefficient of contraction, is determined as the change in volume, per original unit volume, per degree change in temperature.

DENSITY—Defined as mass per unit of volume. For a liquid it may be noted as pounds per gallon and for a solid as pounds per cubic foot.

ESTER—The reaction product of an organic acid and an alcohol in which the organic radical of the alcohol replaces the acid hydrogen of the acid.

EVA RESIN—A copolymer of ethylene and vinyl acetate.

FATTY ACID—A carbon, hydrogen, and oxygen molecule, characterized by a carboxyl group, i.e.,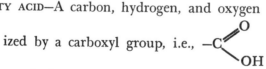

attached to a paraffin-type molecule.

FISCHER-TROPSCH WAX—A synthetic paraffin-type wax produced by catalytic reaction of carbon monoxide with hydrogen.

FLASH POINT—The lowest temperature at which vapors from a substance will continue to burn when ignited by a flame. May be measured by A.S.T.M. test method D-92.

FOLIATION—Production of petals of unburned wax at the periphery of large diameter self-supporting candles.

GAS CHROMATOGRAPHY—An instrumental method for determining carbon number distribution of components in a wax by distillation from a substrate.

GUTTER—The action of excess melted wax running down the outside of a self-supported candle.

HANG-UP—Unburned wax that remains on the wall of jar candles when the candle has expired.

HARDNESS—Resistance a solid substance exhibits toward penetration by a standard object. Hardness of a wax may be measured by needle penetration as described in A.S.T.M. test method D-1321.

HYDROCARBON—An organic compound comprising a skeleton of carbon atoms to which hydrogen atoms are attached.

ISO-PARAFFIN WAX—A highly branched chain paraffin hydrocarbon that melts above room temperature.

MASS SPECTRA ANALYSIS—An instrumental method for measuring the relative abundance of components in a mixture as ionized fragments at low pressure in a magnetic field. For a complete analysis, all components must be vaporizable at operating temperature and pressure. This method is useful in determining the relative abundance of hydrocarbon components in a paraffin wax. A chart showing distribution by carbon number is known as a spectrum.

MELTING POINT—That temperature at which a solid becomes a liquid. Melting point of a wax may be measured by the A.S.T.M. D-87 method or the A.S.T.M. D-127 method.

MICROCRYSTALLINE WAX—A mixture principally of iso-paraffin and cyclo-paraffin hydrocarbons that are isolated from petroleum fractions. In the solid state microcrystalline wax is comprised of small needle-like crystals.

MODULUS OF RUPTURE—A measure of the transverse breaking strength of a wax. May be measured by A.S.T.M. method D-2004.

MOLECULAR SIEVE ANALYSIS—A method in which normal paraffins may be separated from non-normal paraffins by adsorbing normal paraffins from the total sample on molecular pore sized zeolite.

MOLECULAR WEIGHT—The total weight of the atoms present in a molecule relative to an oxygen atom with a weight of 16.00.

NATURAL WAX—A mixture of high molecular weight esters, alcohols, and hydrocarbons of animal or vegetable origin that are solid at room temperature.

OIL—That component of a wax which when isolated from the wax is liquid at room temperature. May be determined by A.S.T.M. method D-721.

ORGANIC SUBSTANCE—A compound or mixture of compounds based

on carbon skeleton molecules of natural or synthetic origin.

PARAFFIN WAX—A mixture of principally straight chain saturated hydrocarbons of petroleum origin that is solid at room temperature.

PETROLEUM WAX—Mixtures of normal paraffins, iso-paraffins, and cyclo-paraffins isolated from petroleum that are solid at room temperature.

POLYETHYLENE—A wax-like high molecular weight hydrocarbon synthesized from the two carbon molecule ethylene. Most polyethylenes have a molecular weight greater than 2000.

SOLUTE—That component in a solution which has been dissolved by the solvent.

SOLVENT—A substance that takes another substance into solution.

SYNTHETIC WAX—A wax-like material made from lower molecular weight components by synthesis, for example Fischer-Tropsch Wax, Polyethylene, and EVA Copolymer.

TAPER—Generally a candle produced by dipping. May be any candle with a gradual reduction in diameter from base to tip.

TENSILE STRENGTH—A measure of the resistance of a wax to be pulled apart. May be measured by A.S.T.M. method D-1320.

TRANSITION TEMPERATURE—That temperature or temperature range at which a wax in cooling from the liquid to the solid state converts from a plastic non-crystalline form to a crystalline one.

VIGIL LIGHT—A small molded candle burned in a glass jar for religious purpose.

VISCOSITY—The resistance that a liquid exhibits to flow, usually determined at a given temperature. Wax viscosity may be measured by A.S.T.M. D-445 method.

VOTIVE LIGHT—A candle casted in a glass jar of such size to provide seven days of burning for religious use.

WAX—A general term for a semi-plastic organic material of vegetable, animal, or mineral origin that is solid at room temperature and melts at elevated temperature.

Conversion Factors

1 Avoirdupois Pound = 453.6 grams
1 Quart   = 946 Cu. cm.
1 Cubic Foot   = 7.48 Gallons
1 Gallon Petroleum Wax = approx. 6.8 Pounds
1 Degree Centigrade = 1.8 Degrees Fahrenheit
1 Degree Fahrenheit = 0.56 Degrees Centigrade

$$\text{Temperature in Centigrade} = \frac{5}{9} \times (\text{F}°-32)$$

$$\text{Temperature in Fahrenheit} = \frac{9}{5} \times \text{C}° + 32$$

1 Atmosphere of Pressure = 14.696 lbs./sq. in.
Centipoise Viscosity = 0.8 × Centistokes Viscosity

See also the charts and graph on the next several pages.

Standard Thermometers for use with Paraffin Wax

A.S.T.M. Test Method	Temp. Range	Immersion	A.S.T.M. Spec. No.
D–87 Melting Point	100 to 180°F	3 1/8 Inches	14 F – 49
D–127 Melting Point	90 to 260°F	———	61 F – 49T
D–938 Congealing Temp.	68 to 212°F	———	54 F – 46T

TEMPERATURE CONVERSION CHART

C°		F°	C°		F°	C°		F°
0	32	89.6	25.6	78	172.4	166	330	626
0.56	33	91.4	26.1	79	174.2	171	340	644
1.11	34	93.2	26.7	80	176.0	177	350	662
1.67	35	95.0	27.2	81	177.8	182	360	680
2.22	36	96.8	27.8	82	179.6	188	370	698
2.78	37	98.6	28.3	83	181.4	193	380	716
3.33	38	100.4	28.9	84	183.2	199	390	734
3.89	39	102.2	29.4	85	185.0	204	400	752
4.44	40	104.0	30.0	86	186.8	210	410	770
5.00	41	105.8	30.6	87	188.6	216	420	788
5.56	42	107.6	31.1	88	190.4	221	430	806
6.11	43	109.4	31.7	89	192.2	227	440	824
6.67	44	111.2	32.2	90	194.0	232	450	842
7.22	45	113.0	32.8	91	195.8	238	460	860
7.78	46	114.8	33.3	92	197.6	243	470	878
8.33	47	116.6	33.9	93	199.4	249	480	896
8.89	48	118.4	34.4	94	201.2	254	490	914
9.44	49	120.2	35.0	95	203.0	260	500	932
10.0	50	122.0	35.6	96	204.8	288	550	1022
10.6	51	123.8	36.1	97	206.6	316	600	1112
11.1	52	125.6	36.7	98	208.4	343	650	1202
11.7	53	127.4	37.2	99	210.2	371	700	1292
12.2	54	129.2	37.8	100	212.0	399	750	1382
12.8	55	131.0	43	110	230	427	800	1472
13.3	56	132.8	49	120	248	454	850	1562
13.9	57	134.6	54	130	266	482	900	1652
14.4	58	136.4	60	140	284	538	1000	1832
15.0	59	138.2	66	150	302	593	1100	2012
15.6	60	140.0	71	160	320	649	1200	2192
16.1	61	141.8	77	170	338	704	1300	2372
16.7	62	143.6	82	180	356	760	1400	2552
17.2	63	145.4	88	190	374	816	1500	2732
17.8	64	147.2	93	200	392	871	1600	2912
18.3	65	149.0	99	210	410	927	1700	3092
18.9	66	150.8	100	212	413	982	1800	3272
19.4	67	152.6	104	220	428	1038	1900	3452
20.0	68	154.4	110	230	446	1093	2000	3632
20.6	69	156.2	116	240	464	1149	2100	3812
21.1	70	158.0	121	250	482	1204	2200	3992
21.7	71	159.8	127	260	500	1260	2300	4172
22.2	72	161.6	132	270	518	1316	2400	4352
22.8	73	163.4	138	280	536	1371	2500	4532
23.3	74	165.2	143	290	554	1427	2600	4712
23.9	75	167.0	149	300	572	1482	2700	4892
24.4	76	168.8	154	310	590	1538	2800	5072
25.0	77	170.6	160	320	608	1593	2900	5252

Interpolation Factors

C°		F°	C°		F°
0.56	1	1.8	3.33	6	10.8
1.11	2	3.6	3.89	7	12.6
1.67	3	5.4	4.44	8	14.4
2.22	4	7.2	5.00	9	16.2
2.78	5	9.0	5.56	10	18.0

VISCOSITY CONVERSION TABLE
(SUS-CSTK)

Saybolt Universal Seconds	Kinematic Viscosity, Centistokes	Saybolt Universal Seconds	Kinematic Viscosity, Centistokes	Seybolt Universal Seconds	Kinematic Viscosity, Centistokes
35.0	2.61	75.0	14.28	175	37.3
36.0	2.92	76.0	14.54	180	38.4
37.0	3.23	77.0	14.80	185	39.5
38.0	3.55	78.0	15.06	190	40.6
39.0	3.88	79.0	15.32	195	41.7
40.0	4.20	80.0	15.58	200	42.8
41.0	4.51	81.0	15.83	210	45.0
42.0	4.82	82.0	16.08	220	47.2
43.0	5.13	83.0	16.33	230	49.4
44.0	5.44	84.0	16.58	240	51.5
45.0	5.75	85.0	16.83	250	53.7
46.0	6.06	86.0	17.07	260	55.8
47.0	6.37	87.0	17.31	270	58.0
48.0	6.68	88.0	17.56	280	60.1
49.0	6.99	89.0	17.80	290	62.3
50.0	7.29	90.0	18.04	300	64.5
51.0	7.59	91.0	18.28	310	66.6
52.0	7.89	92.0	18.53	320	68.8
53.0	8.19	93.0	18.77	330	70.9
54.0	8.48	94.0	19.01	340	73.1
55.0	8.77	95.0	19.25	350	75.2
56.0	9.06	96.0	19.49	360	77.4
57.0	9.35	97.0	19.72	370	79.5
58.0	9.65	98.0	19.96	380	81.7
59.0	9.94	99.0	20.20	390	83.8
60.0	10.22	100	20.5	400	86.0
61.0	10.51	105	21.6	420	90.3
62.0	10.79	110	22.8	440	94.6
63.0	11.07	115	23.9	460	98.9
64.0	11.35	120	25.1	480	103.2
65.0	11.63	125	26.2	500	107.5
66.0	11.90	130	27.3	520	111.8
67.0	12.17	135	28.5	540	116.1
68.0	12.44	140	29.6	560	120.4
69.0	12.71	145	30.7	580	124.7
70.0	12.98	150	31.8	600	129.0
71.0	13.24	155	32.9	700	150.5
72.0	13.50	160	34.0	800	172.0
73.0	13.76	165	35.1	900	193.5
74.0	14.02	170	36.2	1000	215.0

Conversion from CSTK to centipoise: CSTK $\times$ Density = Centipoise

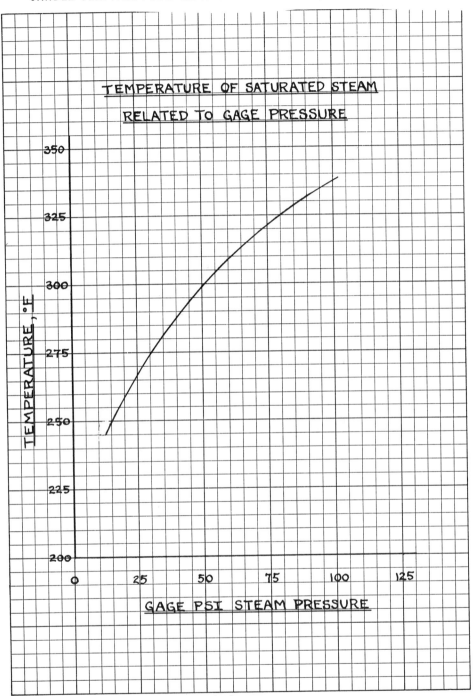

FIGURE 47

Chemical and Equipment Suppliers

Amide U
  Humko Div. of Kraftco Corp.
    White Station Tower, Memphis, Tenn. 38101
Anti-oxidant
  BHT (Butylated Hydroxy Toluene)
    Enjay Chemical Co., 60 W. 49th Street
    New York, N. Y. 10020
  BHA (Butylated Hydroxy Anisole)
    Eastman Chemical Corp., Kingsport, Tenn. 37662
Color Stabilizer
  Tinuvin P: Geigy, Industrial Chemicals Div.
    Saw Mill Rd., Ardsley, New York 10502
Compression Molds
  Hans Kuerschner
    4055 Kaldenkirchen
    Rhineland, West Germany
Dyes
  Patent Chemicals Co., Inc.
    335 McLean Blvd., Paterson, New Jersey
  Leeben Color and Chemical Co.
    103 Lafayette Street, New York, N. Y.
  Pylam Products Co.
    95-10 218th Street, New York, N. Y.
  Morton Chemical Co.
    335 McLean Blvd., Paterson, N. J. 07504
  DuPont Petroleum Chemicals Div.
    Wilmington, Del. 19898
Ethylene-Vinyl Acetate copolymer (Elvax 210)
  E. I. DuPont Co., Wilmington, Del. 19898
Extruders
  Roland Stone Company
    1613 W. Mission Road
    Alhambra, California 91803
  Weber and Seeländer
    333 Helmstedt
    Braunschweiger #17, West Germany
Fischer-Tropsch Wax
  Paraflint: Moore and Munger Company
    33 Rector St., New York, N. Y. 10006
  Ruhrwax: Dura Commodities Corp.
    20 Vesey St., New York, N. Y. 10007
Molds for candles
  Lumi-Craft
    P. O. Box 2, Norwick, Ohio 43767

Early American Candle Company
425 W. Main St., Wescoesville, Pa. 18090
Pourette Manufacturing Company
6818 Roosevelt Way Northeast
Seattle, Washington
Fox Run Craftsmen
1959 Pioneer Rd., Huntingdon Valley, Pa. 19006
George Arold
Orvilla and School Roads, Hatfield, Pa. 19440
Walnut Hill Company
2511 Huntingdon Pike, Huntingdon Valley, Pa. 19006

Perfumes

Felton Chemical Company
599 Johnson Ave., Brooklyn, N. Y. 11237
Magnus, Mabee and Reynard Inc.
16 Desbrosses St., New York, N. Y. 10013
Rhodia Chemical Co., Inc.
60 E. 56th Street, New York, N. Y. 10022

Petroleum Wax

American Oil Co., Division Standard Oil (Indiana)
910 S. Michigan Ave., Chicago, Ill. 60623
Amsco Division, Union Oil of California
Palatine, Illinois 60067
Bareco Div., Petrolite Corp.
6910 E. 14th St., Tulsa, Oklahoma 74115
Boler Petroleum Co.
119 Coulter Ave., Ardmore, Pa.
Cities Service Co.
60 Wall St., New York, N. Y. 10005
Gulf Oil Corporation—Gulf Building,
P. O. Box 2100, Houston, Texas 77001
Humble Oil & Refining Co., Div. Std. Oil Co. (N. J.)
30 Rockefeller Plaza, New York, N. Y. 10020
Industrial Raw Materials Co.
575 Madison Ave., New York, N. Y. 10022
Mobil Oil Company
150 E. 42nd St., New York, N. Y. 10017
Moore & Munger Company
33 Rector St., New York, N. Y. 10006
Shell Companies
P. O. Box 2099, Houston, Texas 77001
Standard Oil of California
225 Bush St., San Francisco, California 94120
Sun Oil Company
1608 Walnut Street, Philadelphia, Pa. 19103

Texaco, Inc.
   P. O. Box 52332, Houston, Texas 77052
Union Oil Co. of California
   Box 7600, Los Angeles, California
Witco Chemical Co., Inc., Sonneborn Division
   277 Park Ave., New York, N. Y. 10017
Plasters
   United States Gypsum Company
      101 S. Wacker Drive, Chicago, Illinois 60606
Polyethylene
   Allied Chemical Co.,
      40 Rector Street, New York, N. Y. 10006
Rubber and Flexible Molding Compounds
   H. V. Hardman, Inc.
      600 Courtland St., Belleville, New Jersey 07109
   The Perma-Flex Mold Company
      1919 E. Livingston Ave., Columbus, Ohio 43209
   General Electric Co., Silicone Products Dept.
      260 Hudson River Rd., Waterford, N. Y. 12188
   Dow Corning Corp.
      Midland, Michigan 48640
Silicone Spray
   Dow Corning Chemical Company
      Midland, Michigan 48640
Stearic Acid
   Humko Div. of Kraftco Corp.
      White Station Tower, Memphis, Tenn. 38101
   Armour Industrial Chemicals Co.
      Box 1805, Chicago, Illinois 60690
Wicking
   Atkins and Pearce Company
      Pearl and Pike Streets, Cincinnati, Ohio 45202
Fox Run Craftsmen
   1959 Pioneer Rd., Huntingdon Valley, Pa. 19006
George Arold
   Orvilla and School Roads, Hatfield, Pa. 19440
Early American Candlecrafters
   425 W. Main Street, Wescoesville, Pa. 18090
Walnut Hill Company
   2511 Huntingdon Pike, Huntingdon Valley, Pa. 19006

Note: The above suggested list of chemical and equipment suppliers for candle production is believed to be correct. It is not to be construed as complete nor as warranty for information on and supply of the indicated chemical or equipment.

Literature References for Additional Reading

Flickering Flames—Leroy Thwing
  Charles E. Tuttle Co., Rutland, Vermont
Colonial Lighting—Arthur H. Hayward
  Dover Publications, Inc., New York, N. Y.
The Chemical History of a Candle—Michael Faraday
  The Viking Press, New York, N. Y.
Modern Art of Candle Creating—Don Olsen and Ray Olsen
  A. S. Barnes and Co., Inc., Cranbury, N. J.
Kitchen Candlecrafting—Ruth Monroe
  A. S. Barnes and Co., Inc., Cranbury, N. J.
Creating and the Art of Blending Colors in Candles—
  Walter Reddig and Mable Atkins
  Lowden Printing Co., Vancouver, Wash.
How to Make Candles and Money—Charles E. Koch
  Borden Publishing Co.,
  1855 W. Main Street, Alhambra, Ca. 91801
How to Know American Antiques—Alice Winchester
  The new American Library of World Literature Inc., N. Y.
The Chemistry and Technology of Waxes—Albin H. Warth
  Reinhold Publishing Corp., New York, N. Y.
Chemistry Made Easy—C. T. Snell and F. D. Snell
  Chemical Publishing Co., Inc., New York, N. Y.
A.S.T.M. Standards on Petroleum Products
  American Society for Testing and Materials
  1916 Race Street, Philadelphia, Pa. 19003
Principles of Chemical Engineering—William H. Walker, Warren
  K. Lewis, William H. McAdams and Edward R. Gilliland
  McGraw-Hill Book Company

Index

201